The Tackle Box Fishing Guide

The Tackle Box Fishing Guide

Philip Barnard

San Diego • New York

A. S. Barnes & Company, Inc.

In London:

The Tantivy Press

The Tackle Box Fishing Guide copyright © 1981 by
A. S. Barnes & Co.

First Edition
Manufactured in the United States of America

For information write to:
A. S. Barnes & Company, Inc.
P.O. Box 3051
La Jolla, California 92038

The Tantivy Press
Magdalen House
136-148 Tooley Street
London, SE1 2TT, England

1   2   3   4   5   6   7   8   9   84   83   82   81

Library of Congress Cataloging in Publication Data

Barnard, Philip.
   The tackle box fishing guide.

   Includes index.
   1. Fishing—Handbooks, manuals, etc.   I.   Title.
SH441.B32   799.1'2   78-69685
ISBN 0-498-02254-4

Contents

Introduction

North American fresh water fishing is probably the best in the world because of the great number of lakes, rivers, and streams. In many regions of the United States and Canada, good sport fishing has become great because of increased knowledge of fish habits and scientific management. There is no guarantee that quality fishing will continue, however, unless interested and responsible people keep local, state, and federal officials informed and active about environmental issues.

Water pollution and habitat destruction are the two biggest obstacles to continued quality fishing, so it is well worth the time and effort of serious fishermen to watch and report what they observe in their own areas. Understanding the nature and requirements of fish will not only help to catch them, but will provide information to keep fishing productive for the future.

The purpose of *The Tackle Box Fishing Guide* is to provide a wide range of the best fishing information on freshwater game fish within a compact format that can be read quickly, and understood easily. Both new and experienced fishermen will find answers to questions that they may have about a particular fish or fishing method in preparation for a fishing trip, and while they are actually fishing.

Fishing tackle, fish habits, fishing methods and conditions are explained in detail, so that fishermen can use their time efficiently and productively. Tackle recommendations are specific but not absolute. They are made to simplify the purchasing of new tackle, and to make it easier for a fisherman to adjust his tackle to a particular type of fishing. Where a wide range of sizes occurs within a species of fish, the tackle recommendations are matched to the average fish rather than to the exceptions.

This guide was written to be used rather than placed on a book shelf and forgotten, so it should be kept in the tackle box, if there is space. Using it will increase the number of fish caught and provide greater fishing pleasure.

Explanation of Terms

BACKING LINE: A line, of equal or greater strength than the regular, placed on the reel spool before the line to partially fill the spool, so that less line is needed, or to make casting and retrieving easier.

BAIT: Fish food in its natural form or cut to fit a hook.

BOTTOM-BUMPING: A method of fishing near the bottom while trolling or casting, in which the bottom is touched by the lure or sinker between each arc in a series of arcs.

BREAKLINE: A gradual or sharp change in bottom condition caused by depth change, vegetation, brushlines, or bottom materials such as rocks.

COMMON MAXIMUM WEIGHT: Based on average weights of fish caught in each of the United States and provinces of Canada. The formula used was: A + ½A = C.M.W. (A = average; C.M.W. = common maximum weight)

COWBELLS: A string of spinners placed ahead of the bait to attract fish.

FAN-CASTING: Casting from a fixed position from one point to another, in a fan-like pattern.

LURE: An imitation of natural food used to attract and catch fish.

MONOFILAMENT: Single-strand fishing line that is exceptionally strong for its diameter.

NORTH AMERICAN RECORD: Rod and reel record for fish caught in North America.

STRUCTURE: Bottom contour of a body of water independent of vegetation or obstacles, such as stumps or rocks.

THERMOCLINE: In northern lakes water stratifies into three layers during the summer. The warm top layer is the *epilimnion*, the middle layer is the *thermocline*, and the cold bottom layer is the *hypolimnion*.

WATER TEMPERATURE ACTIVITY RANGE: The range of water temperatures, from lowest to highest, in which a species of fish feeds actively. It frequently depends upon the temperatures preferred by the prey fishes.

The Tackle Box Fishing Guide

1

Fishing Rods

Fishing tackle should be purchased with a clear purpose in mind because it is easy to buy more than is necessary or to purchase the wrong kinds of equipment. The rod, reel, line, sinkers, and lures should be of the right type and weight to provide optimum fishing action and pleasure. This is known as "balanced" tackle.

Rods

Bargain fishing rods should be avoided unless they are brand names on sale. Quality materials and design can only be guaranteed when the manufacturer is willing to put his name on the product, and the name should be familiar.

A number of points to consider before purchasing a rod are:
- Purpose. (bait casting, spincasting, spinning, fly fishing, trolling, pier fishing)
- Taper and action.
- Weight and length.
- Design and fit of ferrules.
- Design and comfort of handle.

1

- Reel seat locking device.
- Design, hardness, and durability of guides and tips: *ratings*: (1) aluminum oxide or ceramics (2) tungsten carbide (3) chrome stainless steel (4) soft chrome plate.
- Rod material: fiberglass (solid or tubular), bamboo, high-modulus carbon graphite, hybrids.

Tubular glass rods are more expensive than solid glass, but they have the advantage of being lighter and stronger. Split bamboo requires more care than fiberglass and is more expensive and heavier than tubular fiberglass. Graphite is excellent, but sometimes inconsistent in strength (and costly).

Types of Rods

BAITCASTING RODS (offset handle)

Action	Rod length (feet)	Line test (pounds)	Lure weight (ounces)
Ultralight	5 to 6½	2 to 6	1/16 to 1/4
Light	5 to 6½	4 to 10	1/4 to 1/2
Medium	5 to 6	8 to 20	3/8 to 1
Heavy	5 to 6	15 to 25	5/8 to 1¼

SPINCASTING RODS (offset handle)

Action	Rod length (feet)	Line test (pounds)	Lure weight (ounces)
Light	5 to 6½	4 to 10	1/4 to 5/8
Medium	5 to 6	8 to 20	3/8 to 1
Heavy	5 to 6	15 to 25	5/8 to 1¼

SPINNING RODS

Action	Rod length (feet)	Line test (pounds)	Lure weight (ounces)
Ultralight	4½ to 6	2 to 6	1/16 to 1/4
Light	6 to 6½	4 to 10	1/4 to 5/8
Medium	6 to 7½	8 to 17	1/2 to 1¼
Heavy	7½ to 8½	12 to 20	5/8 to 2

FLY RODS

Length (feet)	Weight (ounces)	Level line	Double-taper line	Weight-forward line
6 to 7½	2 to 3	L5F	DT5F or DT5F/S	WF5F
7 to 8½	2½ to 4	L6F	DT6F or DT6S DT6 F/S	WF6F
8½ to 9	3½ to 4½	L7F	DT7F	WF7F/S
8½ to 9	4½ to 4¾	L8F	DT8F	WF8F or WF8F/S
9 to 9½	4¾ to 5	L9F	DT9F	WF9F or WF9F/S
9	5¼			WF10F or WF10F/S

(see page 13 for explanation of abbreviations)

TROLLING RODS (two handed) popular sizes and actions

Action	Rod length (feet)	Line test (pounds)	Lure weight (ounces)
Stiff	4½ to 6½	10 to 20	5/8 to 2½
Stiff	5½ to 6½	20 to 35	1¾ to 3½

PIER RODS (two handed) popular sizes and actions

Action	Rod length (feet)	Line test (pounds)	Lure weight (ounces)
Medium	8 and up	10 to 20	5/8 to 2½
Heavy	8½ and up	14 to 30	1 to 3

2

Fishing Reels

Reels should be balanced to the rods on which they will be used, and reel size, line capacity, and design are important considerations in balancing a reel to a rod. Although baitcasting and spincast rods and reels can be interchanged, they function best when the reel is matched to the rod.

Quality in a reel, or lack of it, shows up in many small ways, so it is important to get a reel made with quality materials, and containing features that provide the easiest and most complete control.

Baitcasting Reels

Features and Characteristics

- Revolving spool with level-wind.
- Adjustable star-drag.
- Easy start and stop in quality reels.
- Gear ratios of 3:1 to 5:1.
- Freespool feature which disengages the gear chain.
- Built-in friction device to prevent overrun.
- Anti-backlash control.

- Light weight for handling and control.
- Minimum clearance between spool end plates to prevent small diameter monofilament lines from catching.
- Heavier versions, with extra features, are made for trolling.

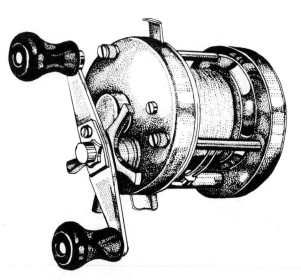

Baitcasting Reel

Spincast Reels

Features and Characteristics

- Enclosed, or partially enclosed spool, line pickup, and release.
- External drag control and adjustment.
- External casting control on line.
- No backlash.
- Gear ratios 3:1 to 5:1.
- Small lures are handled easily.
- The reel sits on top of the rod.
- Loops may slip from spool out of sequence, and cause tangles.

- Line can twist and kink from lure action unless ball-bearing swivels are used with the lures.

Spincast Reel

Spinning Reels

Features and Characteristics

- Open face which permits the line to pull off.
- Mechanical line catcher called a bail.
- Adjustable drag which allows spool to turn prior to breaking point of the line.
- Spools are replaceable for quick line changes.
- Ball-bearing anchor gear train.
- Anti-reverse control, externally operated to prevent reel handle from going out of control from a loose grip or strong fish.
- A skirted reel spool prevents the line from becoming tangled behind the spool.
- No backlash.
- The reel is seated under the rod.
- Loop slippage can result in tangles.
- Swivels should be used to prevent line twists and kinks.

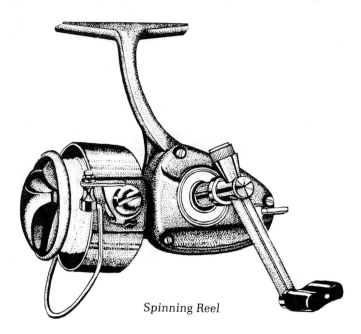

Spinning Reel

Fly Reels

Features and Charactistics: Manually Operated Reel

- Direct drive 1:1 ratios.
- Large diameter.
- Narrow spool.
- Light weight.
- Used primarily as a storage unit for line.
- Reel sits on bottom of the rod.
- Holds about 150 yards of backing line and 30 yards of fly line.

Manual Reel

Features and Characteristics: Automatic Reel

- Usually direct drive 1:1 ratios.
- No handle.
- Release lever for spring power control.
- Usually has clutch to protect fully wound spring from injury.
- Not suitable for large fish.
- Holds about 50 yards of backing line and 30 yards of fly line.
- Reel sits on bottom of the rod.

Automatic Reel

3

Fishing Lines, Leaders, Swivels, Sinkers, Hooks

LINES

Fish have wide-angle vision and can detect motion and shapes from all directions, except directly behind and beneath them. It is generally accepted that fish can not only see fishing lines, but are often frightened by them, or at least wary of them. For this reason a line should be as invisible as possible and no heavier than it has to be for the type of fishing desired.

Braided Lines

Features and Characteristics

- Spreads evenly on a level-wind reel.
- Does not kink or backlash as easily as monofilament line.
- Usually takes strain better than monofilament line.
- Visibility is greater than monofilament line, and should be used with about 6 feet of monofilament leader.
- Basically used for baitcasting on revolving-spool reels.
- Absorbs more water than monofilament.

Monofilament Lines

Features and Characteristics

- Can be used for most forms of spinning, baitcasting, still fishing, and shallow trolling.
- Is less visible than braided line, so may catch more fish.
- Susceptible to kinks, nicks, abrasions, and twists.
- Knots have a tendency to pull loose, so must be checked often.
- Must be stored in a dark, cool place to prevent deterioration.
- Has a relatively high percentage of stretch, but is extremely strong and light for its diameter.
- Rod tips and guides should be kept smooth to prevent abrasions.
- Monofilament should not be tied on hook or lure eyelets that have paint, rust, or roughness on them.
- Monofilament should always be inspected after each snag or bite to prevent line breakage and loss of the lure on succeeding casts.

Fly Lines

Features and Characteristics

- Fly lines are designed to provide weight to the flies during casts, since the flies have very little weight of their own.
- The line should be carefully matched to the rod for smooth and consistent casting.
- *Floating lines* are used with dry flies and bugs for surface fishing.
- *Sinking lines* are used with streamers and other wet flies for fishing near the bottom.
- Fly rods usually have line numbers listed on them for matching line to the rod.
- Fly lines are identified by a letter-number system that describes diameter, weight, and whether or not the line floats or sinks.

Letter symbols (There are also a few variations)

L—level (same diameter for the entire length)
DT—double-taper (tapered at both ends)
WF—weight-forward (heaviest portion at the hook end)
F—floating line
S—sinking line
F/S—floating line with sinking forward section

Number symbols

Line numbers are assigned according to line weights. Number 5 is a light line, and as the numbers get larger, the line gets heavier. Number 10 is about the heaviest used in fresh water fishing.

- The number DT6F means double-tapered, medium-light, floating line.
- The number WF9S means weight-forward, medium-heavy, sinking line.
- *Level line* is the least expensive and is used with wet flies and live bait, but it is awkward to handle.
- *Double-tapered line* is basically a dry fly line which carries the fly well. When the forward section is worn, the line can be reversed.
- *Weight-forward line* makes longer casts possible, especially with wind-resistant lures.

Trolling Lines

Features and Characteristics

- *Metal trolling lines*, for deep trolling, are either braided, twisted, or single strand. They are usually expensive because of greater manufacturing costs.
- Metal line is strong and non-stretch. It is made in tests from 15 to 45 pounds for standard deep trolling in fresh water.
- Metal line is sensitive to strikes and bottom-bumps.
- Metal line has a tendency to kink if it is allowed to unreel too rapidly.

- *Lead-core trolling line*, for deep trolling, has a thin lead core covered with a coating of nylon. It is quite flexible, but has a larger diameter than metal lines.
- *Braided polyester trolling line*, for deep and medium-depth trolling, has less tendency to kink, and is less expensive than metal lines. It is a low-stretch, touch-sensitive line.
- *Monofilament trolling line*, for deep and medium-depth trolling, is low-stretch, and sensitive to strikes and bottom conditions.

LEADERS

Leaders have two basic functions. One is to provide extra strength to the line, and the other is to make the connection between the line and lure as difficult for the fish to see as possible.

Leaders are usually not necessary for most fishing when monofilament line is used, but with or without leaders, the section behind the lure should be checked frequently for frayed spots, especially after a strike or snag.

Wire Leaders

Wire leaders may be made from piano wire, braided wire, or twisted wire, and are generally used to protect the line from the teeth of predatory fish, and from rocks, snags, or other obstacles.

Monofilament Leaders

Most *monofilament leaders* have the purpose of reducing visibility to the line. Monofilament leaders are necessary when braided or fly lines are used. Generally, baitcasting leaders should be about 6 or 8 feet long. Heavy gauge mono-filament leaders, called *shock leaders*, are used in place of wire leaders to reduce visibility.

Fly Leaders

Fly leaders are more critical to the line than other forms of leaders because they affect both the cast and the fish. Length and thickness are important in determining the quality of the casts, and a leader that is too long or too light will collapse during the cast. If it is too short and thick, casting may be easy, but the fish will see it and panic.

Features and Characteristics

- Fly leaders are designed for a variety of conditions and are made in different diameters and lengths, for different purposes.
- Lengths may vary from 6 to over 15 feet.
- Fly leaders must be balanced to the line in thickness and length for proper casting.
- They should be strong enough to hold under pressure, but thin enough so that the fish will not see them.
- Fly leaders of similar sizes and tests do not always match from one manufacturer to another.
- Fly leaders are either level (of equal diameter throughout) or tapered.
- Tapered fly leaders are considered to be easier to handle than level leaders and they disturb the water less.
- The large end of a tapered leader is attached to the line, and the small end is tied to the fly. The small end is the *tippet*.
- Sometimes an extra fine section of tippet is added to the leader to reduce visibility, when fishing in clear water with dry flies.
- Tapered leaders can be made by tying strands of leader material, of decreasing diameters, together.
- Fly leaders with hard, smooth surfaces should be avoided, if they slip when tied, or are too stiff to cast properly.

Size	Test (lbs.)	Tip diam.	Butt diam.	Length (feet)	Hook sizes	Function	Conditions
6X	1½	.005	.017	12	18-22	dry flies	clear, smooth
5X	2	.006	.018	12	14-18		open water
4X	4	.007	.018	9½	12-14	dry flies	clear water
3X	5	.008	.021	7½	8-12	wet flies	clear water,
2X	6	.009	.021	7½	6-8		pools, small streams, riffles
1X	7	.010	.023	6	4-6	heavy bass	cloudy, ac-
0X	8	.011	.023	6	1/0-4	bugs, lures, big flies	tive, deep water

SWIVELS AND SNAP SWIVELS

Swivels perform several functions, but the main one is to prevent the line from twisting. Some lures have a tendency to roll during retrievals and the line would become unmanageable without a swivel.

Other functions of swivels are to attach two lines together, perform as a juncture for combination rigs, and make it easier to change lures. They should be used only when necessary, because they may distract the fish.

Barrel Swivel

Barrel Swivel

Purpose: To join line and leader.

16

Snap Swivel

Snap Swivel

Purpose: To join line or leader to the lure, or to a sinker below a 3-way swivel.

3-Way Swivel

3-way Swivel

Purpose: To join lure to leader and sinker leader. Used in slow trolling where contact with the bottom is desired.

Swivels increase in size as the number decreases. For example, a number 12 is small and a number 2 is much larger.

SINKERS

The basic function of a *sinker* is, of course, to hold the lure or bait under water, but sinkers are designed for specific purposes. The proper sinker can make the difference between catching fish and not catching them. Weight is important, and a sinker should not be any heavier than necessary for its intended purpose.

Pinch-On

Pinch-On

Purpose: For use with or without a bobber in general still fishing.

Split-Shot

Split-Shot

Purpose: For use with light tackle.

Egg   Walker

Slip: Egg, Walker

Purpose: A slip-sinker is used for bottom fishing. It permits the line to slide through the hole while it holds the line on the bottom. A slip-sinker rig is made by first sliding the sinker on to the line. Next, a barrel swivel is attached to the line end. A section of line or leader, about 18 to 24 inches long, is tied to the swivel, and a hook is attached to the end of the leader. The swivel stops the leader from sliding through the sinker, and the bait has freedom to move or be carried by a fish without the weight of the sinker to hinder it.

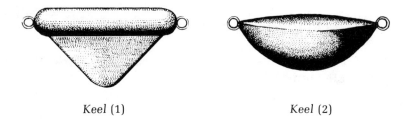

Keel (1)   Keel (2)

Keel: (1), (2)

Purpose: For use in trolling, to prevent the line from twisting, and the lure from snagging. It functions best with a swivel at each end.

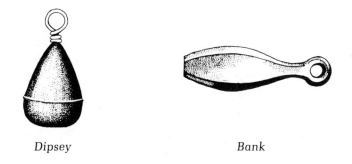

Dipsey   Bank

Slow Trolling: Dipsey, Bank

Purpose: For use in slow trolling or drifting. It is usually tied below a 3-way swivel, and checks the bottom as the bait trails safely above.

Sinkers used with 3-way swivels, for bass and walleyes, are tied about 18 inches below the swivels. Floating lures are attached to leaders, from one to two feet long, behind the 3-way swivels.

Hooks

It is important to use hooks of the best quality available. Inferior hooks do not stay sharp and they may bend or break under stress.

Features and Characteristics

- High quality hooks are made from tempered wire that is neither soft nor brittle.
- Fish hooks are designed for a wide variety of purposes with many variations in eyes, shanks, bends, and barbs.
- The numbering system is not an exact description of different kinds of hooks but only a general one. It works well for general fresh water fishing.
- Hooks are numbered by size—above and below zero. Above zero, hooks increase in size beginning with numbers 1/0, 2/0, 3/0 and ranging upward. Below zero, hooks decrease in size

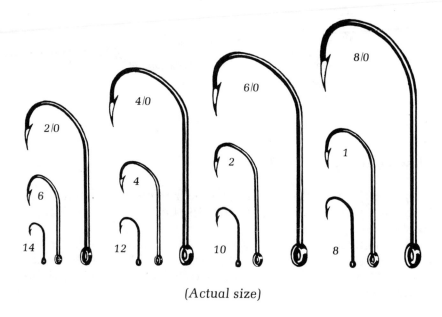

(Actual size)

as the numbers get larger, beginning with 1, 2, 3, and ranging downward.

- A hook of correct size should be used for catching any particular kind of fish. A common mistake is to use a hook that is too large, but if the size is not known, a smaller hook is usually more productive. (See specific fish for hook recommendations in chapter 9.)
- Hook size is influenced by the type of bait, as well as by the size of the fish.
- Regional size differences in fish species should be considered when selecting a hook size from the book suggestions.

4

Lures

Facts About Lures

- The size of a lure is more important than its shape. A lure should be about 1/10 to 1/5 the size of the fish to be caught.
- Fish are sensitive to colors and values (shades). Values and intensities are more important than colors in attracting most fish, and generally, the more natural the better.
- At night, or in murky water, at depths of 8 feet or more, light-colored lures should be used for visibility.
- On clear days with clear water, light-colored lures *decrease* the contrast with the sky and water, and appear more natural when viewed from underneath.
- On overcast days, on dark water, or at night under a light sky, dark surface lures *increase* the contrast with the sky and water, when viewed from below, and have greater visibility.
- A piece of fresh fish or worm, added to a lure as a dressing, will provide an attractive scent to sensitive fish nostrils.
- Lures must be presented to fish at the correct speed to get a reaction. Generally, lures should be retrieved rapidly in shallow water, and slower in deeper water.

- Retrievals should be slower in cool water than in warm, because lower temperatures slow the reactions of the fish.

Plugs (Crankbaits)

Plugs are shaped to resemble small fish and sometimes other animal forms. They are made of wood or plastic, in weights that vary from 1/16 ounce to 3 1/2 ounces or more, and are designed to function at various depths.

Plain snaps, without swivels, are most effective for attaching plugs to lines because they permit free swimming action by the plug. Snaps also provide the convenience of quick plug changes.

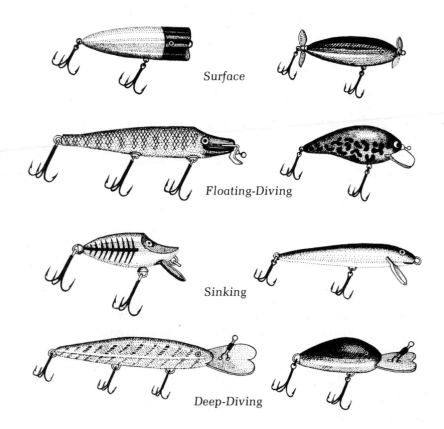

Surface

Floating-Diving

Sinking

Deep-Diving

Facts About Plugs

- *Surface plugs* are made to imitate a variety of surface swimming animals such as mice, frogs, and small fish. A *popper* is a form of surface plug that makes a popping noise as it moves.
- *Floating-diving plugs* float when at rest and dive when they are retrieved. The faster the retrieve, the deeper the dive.
- *Sinking plugs* sink at different rates of speed, and can be fished at different depths or bottom-bumped.
- *Deep-diving plugs* may either float or sink, but are controlled by the speed of the retrievals. They are cast or trolled in deep water.

Spoons

Spoons are made of metal and are designed to imitate the wobbling and darting actions of small fish. They are effective on any fish that preys on baitfish, but sometimes dressed spoons will catch fish that plain spoons will not.

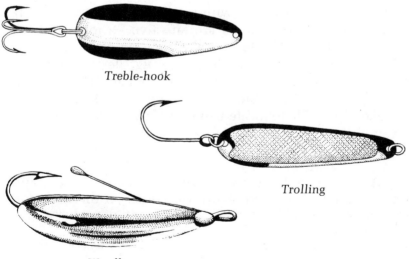

Treble-hook

Trolling

Weedless

Facts About Spoons

- Spoons usually have a single hook attached rigidly, or a single, double, or treble hook attached by a ring for free movement. The rigid hook, sometimes weedless, is used among weeds where a loose hook would foul easily.
- Red and white, black and white, or red and yellow are attractive color combinations to many fish, but metallic colors are more successful with trout and salmon.
- Spoons can be dressed with combinations of pork rind, plastic swimming tails, bucktails, or even fluorescent yarns.
- Spoons should be used with snap-swivels to prevent the line from twisting.
- Small spoons, with a dressing added, can be trolled behind a small boat or canoe to locate panfish and trout.
- Spoons, of the correct size, can be cast from any type of rod except a fly rod. They can be used with a fly rod by allowing the current to carry them along.
- Spoons should be kept in good condition by polishing chipped spots and covering them with clear lacquer. Hooks should be kept sharp.
- Spoons can be retrieved with a variety of movements. Dips, jerks, and jigging actions are effective. A long, fluttering descent attracts salmon and lake trout in deep water.
- *Spoonplugs* are unique, deep-running, deep-diving lures, that can be cast or trolled. They are excellent bottom-bumpers. They are made in a variety of sizes and colors to make it possible to locate fish under a variety of conditions.

Spinners

A *spinner* is basically a swiveled shank, a hook, and a rotating blade. There are many variations on the basic form, and some are combinations of spinners and other lures.

Facts About Spinners

- After they are allowed to sink to the desired depth, spinners are generally retrieved at a steady pace, but if one speed does not catch fish, another should be tried.

- Like spoons, spinners can be trolled behind a small boat or canoe to locate and catch fish. Pork rind, bucktail, or live minnow additions increase the effectiveness of spinners.
- Spinners should be used with snap-swivels to prevent the line from twisting.
- In rivers, spinners should be fished up and across the current, as well as downstream.
- Bass seem to prefer spinners retrieved at a slow pace.
- Trout are attracted to unadorned spinners and spinner-fly combinations.

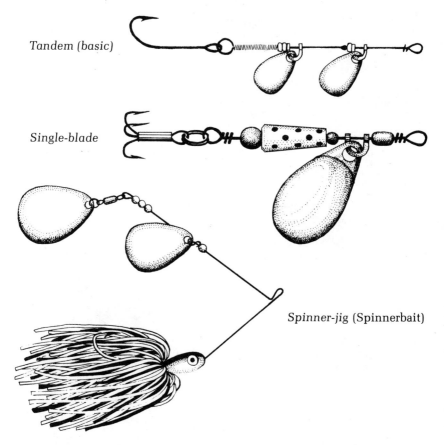

Tandem (basic)

Single-blade

Spinner-jig (Spinnerbait)

Jigs

A *jig* is basically a long-shanked hook with a shaped lead head for balance and weight. The body, or dressing, is made of feathers, hair, or plastic. Tinsel may also be added for flash. Jigs are used to catch a wide range of fishes, thus are made in a wide range of sizes and shapes, from 1/32 ounce to 2 ounces.

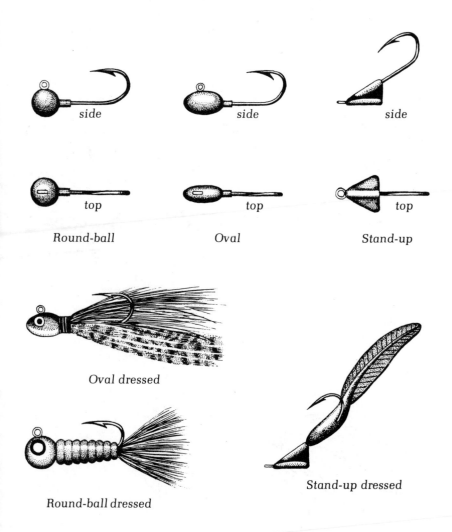

side   *side*   *side*

top   *top*   *top*

Round-ball   Oval   Stand-up

Oval dressed

Stand-up dressed

Round-ball dressed

Facts About Jigs and Jigging

- The *round-ball jig* is for general use. It can be used for a swimming action, hopping on the bottom, or standing on the bottom with a tight line.
- The *oval jig* is useful as a swimmer with slow, steady retrieves that touch the bottom lightly. It is effective in cold water and around snags.
- The *stand-up jig* is designed for bottom fishing in weeds. It sits on the bottom in a vertical position, resulting in greater visibility and movement of the dressing.
- Jigs can be dressed with worms, minnow sections, or pork rind to add scent and action.
- By varying the speed, actions, and depth of a jig, it can be used to catch many different kinds of fishes.
- Basically, jigging involves an up and down movement, but movements can be varied with straight retrieves, starts, stops, dips, and arcs.

Flies

Flies are the smallest of the lures and are constructed to resemble a variety of insects, small crustaceans, and other small creatures. A fly is just a hook to which some material has been attached with thread or cement. Materials used are feathers, hair, chenille, and synthetics. Many fishermen prefer to tie their own flies because of the satisfaction gained, and because they consider these to have a more natural appearance.

Facts About Flies

- *Dry flies* are copies of insects that float on the water surface. They are treated with waterproofing or made of floating materials.
- A dry fly is presented upstream, ahead of, and at an angle to the location of the fish. The fly is then floated over the area.
- *Wet flies* imitate drowned or newly hatched insects attempting to rise to the surface.

Dry Flies

Wet Flies

Nymphs

Terrestrials

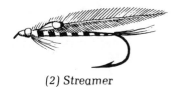

(1) Bucktail   (2) Streamer

(3) Marabou

(1), (2), (3) Basic Streamers

- Wet flies may be presented as dead, live, or as a combination.
- A wet fly is allowed to sink and drift. Action can be provided by jerking the fly toward the surface in short hops, as it drifts or is being retrieved.
- *Nymphs* are imitations of stream larvae, about the time they are ready to hatch into adults.
- Nymphs can be cast upstream, allowed to sink as they drift downstream, then retrieved with a series of jerky motions.
- *Streamers* and *marabous* are made of feathers, constructed to imitate baitfish as much as anything.
- Streamers can be fished across the current, or weighted and fished deep in pools, around rocks, bars, logs, and weeds.
- *Bucktails* are made of hair, usually deer hair, and like streamers they are fished wet and in a similar manner.
- *Terrestrials* are imitations of land insects that have somehow come in contact with the water and become fish food. They include grasshoppers, ants, beetles, worms, larvae, and various flying insects.
- In trout fishing, the size and type of fly to be used is determined more by season and water conditions than by size of the trout.

Pork Rind

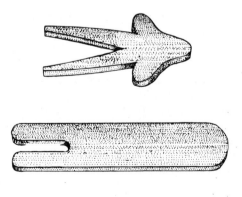
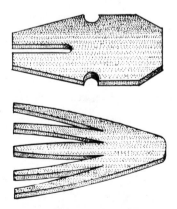

Pork rind can be made from either pig skin or plastic. It comes in a variety of shapes which may resemble anything from a frog to a worm, and can be used as a dressing for other lures or by itself. Pork rind should be preserved only in salt brine, not formaldehyde, because fish are repelled by chemical odors.

Plastic Bait Imitations

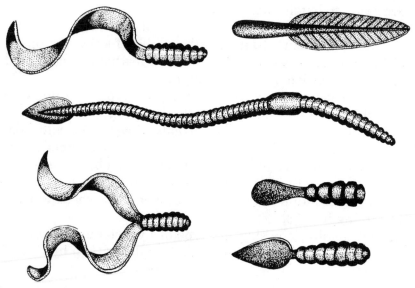

Plastic Bait Imitations

Plastic lures are made to resemble real and imaginary creatures. Used with the right methods they are excellent for attracting fish, and are particularly effective when they are used as dressing for spoons, spinners, and jig heads. Plastic worms can be cut into short segments, placed on small hooks, and used to catch panfish.

5

Baits

Facts About Baits

- Natural baits should move naturally, be attached properly, and be fresh.
- Live *minnows* are most effective for still fishing. Dead ones are used for casting and trolling.
- A live minnow, fished without a float or sinker, has freedom to move and attract fish, but at times split-shot may be necessary to hold the minnow at the depth desired.
- Live minnows should be hooked in the tail or under the dorsal fin above the backbone, to keep them alive as long as possible. If they are hooked through the lips, care must be taken not to puncture the skull, or close the mouth and prevent breathing.
- *Worms* should be active to be attractive to fish. They can be hooked in the end opposite the "collar," to avoid injury and to insure activity.
- *Insects* can be tied to a hook with a piece of thread wrapped around the thorax, between the legs. This keeps them alive and active.

Earthworm Care

Commercial earthworms are kept refrigerated until they are sold because they will not survive for very long except between temperatures of 45 and 55 degrees Fahrenheit. Unfortunately for the worms and the fisherman who buys them, they are frequently removed from the refrigerator and placed in a hot automobile, or in direct sunlight. First the worms become inactive and then they die. Overheated earthworms, still alive, droop over the hook unable to move. In that condition they do not attract fish, but overheating can be prevented by using the materials and procedures listed below.

Materials

- An insulated container about 12" x 18" x 12". (Styrofoam is excellent.) Air holes are required.
- A plastic container for the worms about 8" x 8" x 6". (Metal cans should not be used. They concentrate the cold and chill the worms.)
- One or two refreezable ice packs.
- A jar of water. (Allow it to stand 48 hours to eliminate all traces of chlorine.)
- Peat moss for worm bedding. (Available at garden supply stores.)
- Newspaper.
- Thermometer.

Procedures

1. Fill the small plastic worm container with peat moss to a depth of 4 inches.
2. Mix just enough water with the peat moss to dampen it.
3. Test the mixture by squeezing a handful as hard as possible. If water drips out, the mixture is too wet. Add dry peat moss until the excess water is absorbed.
4. Check the depth of the damp peat moss and be sure it does

not exceed 4 inches. The limited depth allows air to circulate around the worms.

5. Place a layer of damp newspaper, 3 or 4 sheets thick, on the top of the peat moss.

6. Wrap the ice packs in several thicknesses of newspaper and place them in the insulated container. The newspaper prevents the worm box from coming into direct contact with extreme cold.

7. Place the worm box in the insulated container and cover the outside box.

8. Acquire the worms. If you buy them, check them thoroughly. If the worms do not squirm in your hand, do not accept them. Ask for fresh worms or go someplace else.

9. Spread the worms on a damp newspaper to separate them from their old bedding. Be sure they are in complete shade. A few seconds of direct sunlight can put them into shock because sunlight to an earthworm is like scalding water to us.

10. Place the worms on the top of the new bedding, but do not replace the damp newspaper cover. The outside box cover can be replaced. Healthy worms will burrow into the new bedding while the sick ones will remain on top.

11. Allow a few minutes for the healthy worms to burrow down, then remove any worms that remain on top of the bedding. Sick worms contaminate healthy ones. An 8″ x 8″ x 6″ worm box will hold about 50 average worms or about 15 nightcrawlers safely.

12. Place the damp newspaper cover over the worm box and close the outside container. Keep it in the shade at all times and check the thermometer occasionally. Keep the temperature between 45 and 55 degrees Fahrenheit.

Earthworms will last for four or five days with proper care. Keep the temperature under control, the bedding damp, and sprinkle a little cornmeal on the top to feed the worms. Any long term storage requires special food, special containers, special bedding, and special knowledge.

Long Term Earthworm Care

An alternative to specialized, long term care is to dig a patch of ground that is in shade at least half the day.

Procedures

1. Dig a patch about 2' x 2' x 18" deep.
2. Add enough peat moss to loosen the soil. Mix well.
3. Add only enough water to moisten the soil, not soak it.
4. Place the worms on the ground while the patch is in full shade. Cover lightly with soil after removing dead worms.
5. About once a week sprinkle the patch with a light layer of mulch or chopped vegetable scraps and a little cornmeal.
6. Keep the soil damp but not soaked. Cover if necessary.

If the conditions are suitable within the patch, the worms will remain in it and will be available for future use. If the conditions are not quite right, the worms are free to move into the surrounding soil and avoid any contamination that might occur from sick worms or toxic conditions.

Minnow Care

Two things must be considered in keeping minnows alive after they are purchased. These are *water temperature* and *oxygen supply*. Fish have very little tolerance to quick temperature changes, so if they are taken from water with one temperature and placed in water of another with a noticeable difference, they will die of shock. Most fish can tolerate gradual temperature changes within 10 to 15 degrees, but different species have different ranges.

The water temperature of minnows or other baitfish should be kept as close to the tank temperature as possible. This can only be done if the minnows are bought near the place where they are to be used, or if they are cooled with ice.

Minnows should be carried in a two-piece minnow bucket with a perforated inner section. The standard bucket will hold a dozen minnows comfortably, but they must be provided with oxygen almost immediately, until they are removed from the outer container and placed in circulating water. Unless the bucket is equipped with a pump, oxygen is provided by pouring water back and forth into the bucket. A kitchen basting syringe will also supply oxygen almost as well as a pump, but any hand method is inconvenient compared to the use of oxygen tablets which can be added to the water.

Before the perforated bucket liner is placed in a river or lake, the water must be tested with a hand. If the temperatures of the bucket water and the river water are close, which they usually are not, the bucket liner can be placed in it. If the two water temperatures are more than a degree or two apart, the whole bucket is placed in the water until the two temperatures are equal, or water is added gradually from the lake or stream to the minnow bucket.

The lake water should not be permitted to mix directly with the bucket water until the temperatures are equal, because of the possibility of shock. Oxygen must be supplied continuously, as long as the minnows are restricted to the bucket water.

Unless the air is cool, minnows should be kept in shade to prevent the water from heating. This is true even when the minnows have lake or river water circulating around them, because surface water warms rapidly in direct sunlight.

Handling minnows with an aquarium net is much less damaging to them than grabbing them with a hand. The hand causes panic and bruising as the minnows bump the sides of the bucket to escape.

6

Fishing Knots

The right fishing knot can do much to save lures, fish, and in some cases, the entire line. Knowing what knot to use and how to tie it, makes fishing more efficient and consequently more enjoyable. The *universal knot* is derived from traditional knots and can be used, in one form or another, for most fresh water fishing purposes.

Universal Knot

Purpose: To tie a line to a hook, lure, swivel, or reel.

Method

(1) Place the line through the hook-eye and extend the end about 6 to 8 inches. (2) Make a loop with the line end. Hold it with the left thumb and forefinger at point A. (3) Wrap the line end around the doubled line six times. (4)(5) Hold the hook, and with the other hand, pull the line end until the turns are snug. (6) While holding the hook, pull the main line with the other hand until the knot is tight against the hook-eye. (7) Clip the line end close to the knot.

39

Steps for tying a Universal Knot

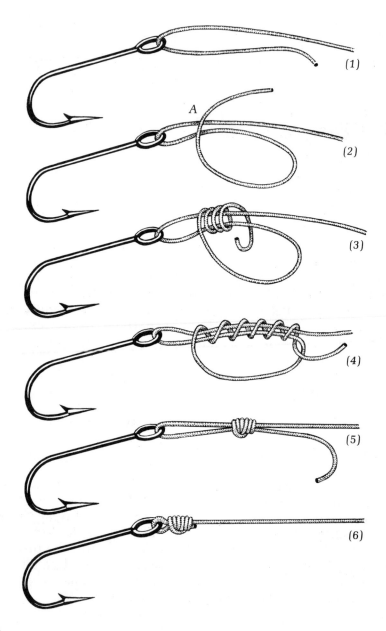

A

(1)

(2)

(3)

(4)

(5)

(6)

Universal Loop Knot

Purpose: To permit the lure to move freely and naturally through the water.

Method

(1) Tie an overhand knot about 9 inches from the line end. (2) Extend the line end through the lure-eye, to about ¾ inch from the knot, point A. Hold the line at point B, form the universal knot and wrap six times. (3) Grip the entire knot firmly in the left hand, point B, and pull the line end slowly, so that the loops tighten evenly around the line, ahead of the overhand knot. (4) Tighten the universal knot by pulling the line end with pliers. (5) Slide the universal knot until it is against the overhand knot by pulling on the main line while holding the lure. (6) Clip the line end close to the knot.

Steps for tying a Universal Loop Knot

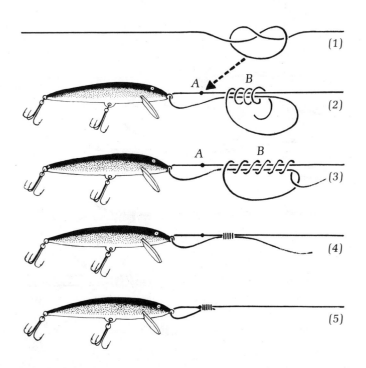

Universal Line Knot (1)

Purpose: To tie one line to another.

Method

(1) Cross line B over line A with the line ends extending about 6 to 8 inches from the crossover. (2) Make a loop with

Steps for tying a Universal Line Knot (1)

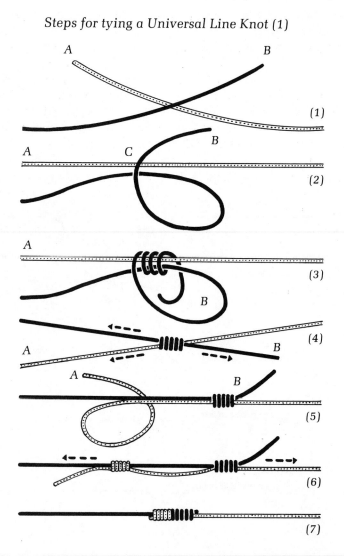

line end B, and hold the line at point C between the left thumb and forefinger. (3) Wrap line B around line A six times. (4) Tighten the knot by pulling line B and line end A in one direction, and line end B in the opposite direction. (5) Form a loop with line end A, wrap it around line B six times, and pull tight. (6) Pull both main lines in opposite directions to bring the knots together. (7) Clip line ends close to the knots.

Universal Line Knot (2)

Purpose: To tie two lines together, or a line and leader of different thicknesses.

Method

(1) Double back the lighter of the two lines, line B, 6 to 8 inches, and form the regular universal knot. Wrap the doubled line B around line A only 3 times, and tighten it. (2) Form the universal knot with the heavier line A, wrap it around line B six times, and tighten it. (3) Pull the doubled line B and line A in opposite directions to bring the knots close together. (4) Clip the line ends close to the knots.

Steps for tying a Universal Line Knot (2)

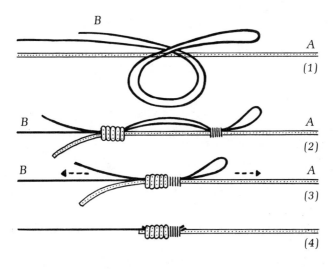

43

Universal Fly Line Knot

Purpose: To tie a leader to a fly line.

Method

(1) Form a universal knot with the leader B, and wrap it around the fly line end A, 4 times. (2) Pull the leader B and its end in opposite directions to tighten the loops. Pull slowly while pushing the loops together with a thumb nail. (3) Tighten the knot by holding the leader and pulling the end with pliers, so that the knot grips into the soft coating of the fly line. (4) Clip the line ends close to the knot.

Steps for tying a Universal Fly Line Knot

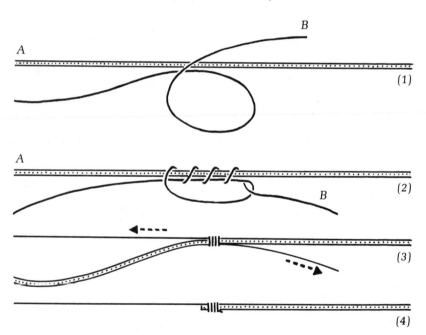

7

Depth and Temperature Indicators

Depth finders are electronic instruments which are of particular value for fishing on large or unfamiliar bodies of water. The bottom structure of a body of water can be determined and analyzed for fish locations as the boat moves over the water in a pre-determined pattern. Depth finders are designed to function within specific ranges, so should be selected for depths that match the depths for which they will be used.

A dial is the basic feature for indicating depth on all models, but other features may include a sound signal and a graph recorder that provides a printout of bottom structure and fish location.

The complex *fish finders* and *structure interpreters* may have four range controls for operating at different depths, and two modes on the recorder unit. Together they provide eight close-up increments.

Chart pictures can be produced that show fish and bottom structure in good detail. The chart paper control may have several speeds to function with different boat speeds.

Prices vary according to function and features, so several types should be checked before purchasing one.

Depth thermometers are less expensive than depth finders and are valuable tools in locating the preferred water temperatures of fishes.

A low-cost combination thermometer-depth finder sells for just a few dollars. It is lowered into the water on a line, and water is trapped in a cylinder. Water pressure is registered on a gauge along with temperature. The pressure indicates the depth.

The more expensive electronic depth thermometers operate with a probe suspended from a wire. The temperatures are read from a dial.

A battery operated, oxygen-temperature probe is also available that provides a direct readout of oxygen content and water temperature.

8

Fishing Information

Fish Populations

When fishing has been good for several years in a particular place, it is easy to believe that it will continue forever. But changing conditions can drastically change fish populations in a short period of time.

Gradual build-up of silt may make bottom and water conditions unfavorable to fish that need cool, clear, deep water with a sand and gravel bottom. These same conditions may be favorable to fish such as catfish.

Winter freezeouts on shallow lakes may kill many of the fish, and change the percentages of those that survive. Heavy wave action during spawning season may destroy egg clusters, or parasites, such as the sea lamprey, may reduce fish populations, as they did with the lake trout in the Great Lakes.

Alterations of the land and water by construction, pollution, or by the introduction of alien species such as carp, have had a serious impact on fish habitat and fish populations.

In sport fishing it is not common for a highly productive area to be over-fished, but it can happen. Over-fishing may combine with changes in the habitat to hasten the losses in fish populations, but only a single condition may be blamed.

Usually over-fishing occurs in species that are at the top of the food chain, such as largemouth and muskellunge, because they are fewer in numbers and larger than other fishes. They also require more territory. These differences make them more vulnerable to over-fishing and to habitat changes.

Uncontrolled commercial fishing can do great damage to fish populations, and has done so in the Great Lakes at times, and to the oceans as well. Until the United States extended its territorial waters to include the Grand Banks off the northeast coast, cod fishing was being destroyed by over-fishing from foreign fleets.

At one time it was widely believed that the oceans could provide an unlimited supply of food for the world, but this belief is no longer held by most marine biologists who have studied the situation.

Under some circumstances, interference seems to be exactly what is required. Native fish, such as yellow perch, may overpopulate a lake and become stunted from a lack of food. By introducing predator fish such as northern pike, the perch population can be controlled. The perch grow larger from less competition, and the northern pike thrive on the abundance of food.

Probably the most successful example of constructive human interference has been in the Great Lakes, where coho, chinook, and other salmon have been introduced. They have thrived on a plentiful supply of alewives that came into the lakes from the Atlantic Ocean through the St. Lawrence Seaway, but pollution is a severe problem.

The sea lamprey also came through the Seaway to the Great lakes, and almost succeeded in destroying the lake trout by attaching themselves to the trout and living on their blood. Fortunately, control programs have prevented the lampreys from continuing their destructive patterns, but the lake trout populations have not yet recovered completely.

Over the years, the states bordering on the Great Lakes have conducted poisoning programs that kill the lamprey larvae in the streams where they hatch. The poison is selective and kills only the lampreys, but it is expensive and must be continued indefinitely.

Newer control methods are being developed that may be

cheaper and better. One such method is water temperature control at specific locations with the use of waste water from power plants.

Since changes can be beneficial to one species of fish and harmful to another, all man-made changes in fish habitats should be studied thoroughly before action is taken.

Weather Conditions

- During the summer months, fish generally stay in deeper water during the day and in shallower water at night. As surface water temperature rises during the day, the fish seek out cooler water. At night when the surface water cools again, the fish may move into the shallows.
- Fish usually stratify during the summer according to size. The larger the fish the deeper it goes.
- In spring and fall, fish may come into the shallows during the day because the water surface may be heated by the sun. At night the deeper water may be warmer than the surface, so the fish return to it.
- In the summer, fish are usually found in shady places, except on overcast days when they may range further.
- Wind direction affects wave action and water temperature. In the spring, fish often congregate along the shore from which the wind is blowing, because the wind circulates the warm water up from the bottom and the fish are attracted to it.
- A cold front will push fish into deeper water for several days.
- If the water is cloudy or the day overcast, fish usually can be located in shallower water than usual.

Locating Fish

- Fish are usually near the water surface or in deep water, but they are sometimes suspended in the middle zones.
- Fish can often be found near weeds that extend parallel or perpendicular to the shore where the breakline occurs.
- Fish do not usually stay in one place for long periods of

time. Therefore, if there is no action in one place another should be tried.

- Small fish are often good indicators of larger fish. The larger ones will be deeper.
- If largemouth bass are located at one depth, walleyes can often be found several feet below them, perhaps at double the depth.
- Bottom conditions are indicators of fish habitats. Vegetation, mud, sand, gravel, rocks, logs, drop-offs, bars, spring-holes, inlets, and currents have an influence on where fish are.
- A notebook and a contour map are valuable additions to a tackle box. Catches, locations, conditions, and methods are worth keeping records on for future reference.

Fishing Tips

- Fish can be located in lakes by fan-casting or by slow trolling at varying depths. Deep running lures can be bottom-bumped to get information on the structure and depth of the area.
- Lures should be kept off soft bottoms because they stir up the muck and usually frighten the fish.
- Bottom-bumping is an effective method for catching fish where the bottom is hard. The lure is permitted to touch bottom, then is lifted in an arc and allowed to touch bottom again. This process is repeated over the fishing zone. Sinking lures such as spoons, deep-diving plugs, or a floating plastic worm rigged on a keel sinker and leader are successful.
- Whenever the line suddenly goes slack after a strike, the fish is moving toward the fisherman with the lure. The slack should be taken up quickly and the hook set.
- Shallow running lures can be maneuvered over and around weed edges.
- Each different species of water plant requires a different fishing method because of the difference in "feel" and toughness.

- Under most conditions it is better to keep a boat moving because fish are usually moving from one place to another, however slowly. A boat should only be anchored when a concentration of fish are located, and then only toward deep water, away from the fishing area.
- Lures and baits should match the available natural foods.
- When spinning or spincast reels are being used, a fish should be retrieved with a "pumping" action. The rod tip is lifted to pull the fish in and as it is lowered the line is reeled in. Reeling against the pull of the fish causes the clutch to slip, which in turn causes the line to twist.
- A large fish should not be landed by force. It should be thoroughly tired before landing is attempted, at which time a net or gaff should be used.
- Sudden motions and bright clothing can be seen by fish from 50 to 100 feet away, if the water is smooth. Clothing should be in neutral colors and shades.
- Talking will not disturb fish, but vibrations caused by bumping the boat, scraping feet, or banging the tackle box will.
- An old piece of carpet on the bottom of the boat will muffle sounds.
- Time can be saved and noises avoided if the tackle box is kept within easy reach, and if it is organized for the type of fishing to be done.
- Rough or rusty hooks should be discarded, and rough or rusty lure eyelets kept in shape by filing with a small rat-tail file, coarse first, then fine.
- An end loop knot will cause less concentrated friction on the line than a tight knot.
- A nail clipper is an excellent tool for trimming knot ends.

Lake Fishing

The location of fish in lakes depends upon season, water temperature, vegetation, angle of the sun, land forms, water depth, time of day, fish characteristics, bottom conditions, wind direction, food supplies, clarity of the water, weather conditions and other factors.

During the summer, fish come into shallow water in the early morning or late afternoon and evening. In the middle of the day they move into deep water to escape the heat. If the day is overcast or the water choppy, fish may also stay in shallow water.

In spring and fall, the surface water warms in the daylight hours on sunny days, and fish migrate toward the shallows. At night, when the surface water cools, they return to deep water.

The structure and conditions of the lake bottom are of particular importance in locating fish. Bars, sloping points, drop-offs, weed bed edges, logs, rocks, spring holes, inlets, sand and gravel bottoms, are the places where fish gather.

Lakes, in which extremes of temperature occur during the winter months, develop thermal stratification during the summer months. The top layer is the *epilimnion*, which is the warmest. The *thermocline* is under the epilimnion and is cooler. Most fish stay within the thermocline during the day. The coldest layer is the *hypolimnion,* which is under the thermocline.

Since it is difficult to remember and locate lake structure from a moving boat, it is always good practice to use marker buoys and a contour map, in addition to a notebook, for accurate repeated runs. Fish may move from their usual deep water location toward shallow water only once or twice a day, or they may become active and remain in deep water, where they are most of the time. Therefore, the more information a fisherman has about conditions and lake structure, the better his chances are for catching fish.

River Fishing

Water conditions may vary considerably from one river to another and from a river to a lake. River water is frequently cloudy to one degree or another, and the differences between surface water and deep water are minimal because of the constant circulation. Oxygen content may be greater because of water activity.

Fast rivers differ considerably from slow, sluggish rivers. Oxygen content is much higher in faster rivers, and bottoms are usually sand, gravel, and rock. The bottoms of slow rivers are usually covered with sediment.

The species and location of fish that inhabit a river are determined by the volume of water, its speed, water temperature, vegetation, bottom conditions, food supply and other factors. The cold, clear, swift water of small, spring-fed streams can only support fish such as trout, which can tolerate cold water, and which can live on the insects and small crustaceans that are available as food.

Large bottom feeders, such as catfish, carp, and paddlefish, usually are found in mature rivers, where the water volume is great but where the speed of the water is not so great that it prevents sediment from settling to the bottom. Under these conditions most predatory fish cannot exist because of the scarcity of small fish to feed upon. Most of the fish that do exist there live on the nutrients they get from the sediment.

Bushes, logs, over-hanging trees, pools, and rocks may all be locations for fish in rivers. A careful examination of a river's structure will usually indicate where the fish will be and what kinds of fish can be found there.

River fishing for walleyes, smallmouth bass, and crappies is usually done with controlled drifting, which allows the fisherman to make short casts into the cover areas as the boat passes. Spinning or spincast tackle functions well under these conditions if a line of about 8 pound test is used. A lighter line will break too easily, and a heavier line will be more difficult to use with the small lures that are preferred. Small lures that imitate natural foods, in brown or yellow and weighing 1/16 to 1/8 ounce, seem to be most attractive to predatory river fish. Small jigs, dressed with a piece of nightcrawler to provide scent, are productive.

Lures should be retrieved slowly in rivers because the movement of the water will keep them active. A fast retrieve will not permit a lure to get to the bottom, where it should be to reach the fish. Casting across the current and upstream will give a lure the chance to sink. A lure has a better chance than bait because it is more durable and will not break away on quick casts or against rocks. Spoons and spinners are effective because of the action and flash in cloudy water.

Fishing in Weeds

Successful fishing in weeds requires a knowledge of the basic types of weeds and special fishing techniques. The feel and strength of weeds varies with the species, and by learning the differences, they are easier to cope with. Frequently the fisherman is not aware that his hook is fouled, or he mistakes the weeds for a fish. In either case fishing is more difficult and time consuming.

Some lures and hooks are designed to avoid weeds and should be used. Perhaps the best lure is a stand-up jig with a tapered head and the hookeye on the tip. A floating plastic body attached to the hook will remain visible to the fish while the jig is on the bottom.

A jig should be brought up from the bottom in a swimming motion. It is arced from one place to another wherever small openings appear, and can be fluttered during the arcs.

A nightcrawler or plastic worm can be jigged or cast into the tops of the weeds and allowed to sink for a distance before it is pulled up and across the top of another patch. This process is repeated from one patch to another wherever small openings appear. The same technique can be used with a spinner or a spinner-night crawler combination.

Plastic or live nightcrawlers can also be fished from the bottom with a slip-sinker rig, which allows the fish to move with the bait without the weight of the sinker holding it back. This method is effective in openings and at weed edges.

The edges of weed beds are usually the most productive, so by moving into them, back out, into them and back out in a pattern, thorough coverage of an area can be made. Weeds should be fished closely, early and late in the day, and on overcast days. If the fish cannot be located, they are probably in deeper water.

Trolling

Trolling is a productive method for locating fish, but it requires preparation. A contour map should be marked with the locations of weed beds, bars, stumps, brush, points, drop-offs, channels, migration routes, and any other structural reference points. Where structure is not visible, buoy markers made from plastic bottles can be used.

Except on large bodies of water where the water can get rough, small boats and small motors are better for trolling than larger ones. Small boats can be stopped quickly when fish are hooked or the lure is snagged, and in general they are more maneuverable.

If there are fish in an area, the speed and depth of the lure are two main factors in determining whether or not they will be caught. Speed and depth are guided by lure action, water conditions, and weather, but the most direct approach is to vary the speeds until the fish respond. Wherever bottom conditions are firm and free of brush, the lure can be bumped on it to check water depths and find the location of the fish.

Trolling takes practice because of the variations in bottom structure. Unless bottom conditions are familiar, time is wasted in trying to adjust to them. Snags are common, so a lure-saver is helpful. A lure-saver is a weighted ring that snaps around the line, sinks to the lure, and is pulled off the snag with the attached cord.

Back Trolling

Back trolling is an effective method for covering fishing structure from about 10 to 30 feet deep. The boat is usually backed into the wind to control drift. By following an "S" or "snake" pattern, both deep and shallow water can be covered in a continuous sweep along a breakline while trolling slowly.

Backing into the wind can be alternated with controlled drifting on the returns with the wind. Controlled drifting can also be used for trolling or casting while moving in one direction along a breakline.

Spinning tackle is basic to back trolling and drift trolling. A slip-sinker rig, in combination with an open reel bail, permits the bait to be carried by a fish with a minimum of resistance. When the bait is taken, the boat can be "hovered" in position. "Hovering" is also useful when water depths are being checked.

Tackle

SPINNING: Medium action rod with 8 to 10 pound test line, or heavy action rod with 10 to 14 pound test line.

55

RIGGING: (in order of attachment to line) Egg, or bell slip-sinker, swivel, 18 to 24 inch leader, hook.
BAITS: Minnows, nightcrawlers.

Shallow Trolling

Trolling patterns can be determined by visible reference points. The boat should be maneuvered as close to them as possible.

In shallow trolling, the tackle depends upon the kind and size of fish to be caught, but standard tackle is limited to about 7 feet of water. Standard tackle has limited reel capacity, too much rod flexibility, and line that stretches. Extensions of lines are limited to about 80 feet because they become insensitive beyond that.

Tackle

BAITCASTING: Medium action rod with 8 to 15 pound test line and small lures.
SPINNING: Medium action rod with 8 to 15 pound test line and small lures.
FLYCASTING: Floating line, system No. 8 or more. Flies in sizes 6 to 12.
LURES: Small spoons, spinners, sub-surface and deep-running plugs, jigs with pork rind strips, plastic worms, all used with snap-swivels. Flies in tandem.

Middle Depth Trolling

Trolling in an area with a variety of structural patterns and changing depths can be difficult. Large reservoirs in particular have bottom conditions that require careful study. Under difficult conditions, trolling cannot be done efficiently without a depth finder.

Although water temperature and time of day are important factors in indicating where fish might be, trolling can begin in shallow water as close to the shoreline as possible. Small, shallow-running lures are used at this stage, and if no fish are caught, deeper-running lures can be used over the same area. Deeper lures should also be bottom-bumped so the depths and conditions can be checked.

Any fish that are caught are indicators of other, perhaps larger, fish. Consequently, drop-offs, points, bars, and other structures should be covered in the immediate area. Marker buoys can be placed at key depths and structure boundaries.

Middle depth trolling ranges from about 7 to 25 feet and requires up to 60 or 80 yards of line. Specialized tackle is necessary because of water resistance and the amount of line required.

Tackle

TROLLING: Short, stiff rod, level-wind reel with 150 to 200 yard capacity and star drag, non-stretch trolling line from 12 to 20 pound test. Non-stretch line is sensitive to bottom conditions and strikes, and the short, stiff rod compliments it. The combination is also useful for yanking snagged plugs away.
LURES: Spoons, plugs, spinners in various sizes, used with snap-swivels in sizes No. 2 or No. 3

Deep Trolling

In deep trolling, a depth-finder and depth thermometer are basic tools. Salmon and lake trout are the fish usually sought, so the discussion will be limited to them.

Before deep trolling can begin, it is important to know how deep weights of 1, 2, 3, 4 ounces or more run at line lengths of 25, 50, 75, and 100 yards. Weight running depths can be determined by starting in deep water and trolling into shallow at a set trolling speed and line length. When the weight hits bottom, the depth is recorded and the run is continued with the next line length. The most efficient method is to test a single weight through all the line lengths, beginning with the heaviest weight and longest line section, and working down to the lightest weight. With this system, a single run can be made with each weight with stops for adjustments and record keeping.

Terminal tackle can be rigged in several ways, but a flexible system is made with a 3-way swivel, dropper weights in various sizes, and weight leaders in lengths of 2 to 6 feet for controlling lure distance from the bottom. The leaders should have snap-swivels at both ends for quick changes. The leader to the lure should not exceed the rod length—for ease of handling when the line is reeled in.

When depths and water temperatures have been checked and the correct weight attached to the 3-way swivel, the speed of the troll is set by watching the lure action in shallow water. Speed must be watched closely, but slight variations in the basic speed can increase the attractiveness of the lure for short intervals.

Pumping the rod at intervals can increase the chances of hooking a fish. The changes in lure action excite some fish into striking. When a fish hits the lure, steady pressure is all that is necessary to set the hook. Jerking may tear the hook loose.

The drag should be set lightly and kept there. Control of a fish is a matter of steady pressure, whether the fish is running with the lure or being reeled in. It should not be overpowered nor allowed to run freely. It should be given plenty of time to tire under steady pressure; then it cannot lunge and break loose.

Downrigger fishing is another way to fish deep. Downriggers consist of a reel, a cable, and a weight. Depths can be controlled exactly, and when the fishing line is attached to the weight, the lure extends straight out behind the boat rather than at an angle. When a fish is hooked, the line is released from the weight and the fisherman handles the fish directly.

Tackle

DEEP TROLLING: A short, two-handed, medium-heavy action rod with roller guides, or tungsten carboloy guides and a roller tip. Large capacity, level-wind reel with a star drag, holding up to 200 yards of metal line of 20 to 30 pound test.

LURES: Large fluorescent spoons in combinations of red, yellow, green, black, nickel, blue, gold, bronze, brass, copper. Plugs, spinners, and cowbells are also effective. Variety pays.

SINKERS: 1, 2, 3, and 4 ounces or more.

Playing the Fish

When a fish is hooked, it usually will attempt to dash toward cover. The tip of the rod should be held in an almost vertical position, regardless of what direction the fish might go. In this position it is possible to keep the fish under control. If the fish is strong enough to pull the rod tip down, line should be released while keeping an even tension on it. When the fish stops, the rod tip should be raised again. Any slack in the line caused by a change in the direction of the fish should be reeled in immediately. A loose line provides the fish with an opportunity to escape either by throwing the hook or snapping the line. Too much tension on the drag can also result in a broken line, so the fish should be thoroughly tired before any attempt is made to land it.

A spinning rod should be pumped and reeled only on the downstroke. In this way a twisted line can be avoided. The fish is pulled in on the upstroke. The forefinger of the hand holding the rod can be used as a variable drag, easily adjusted by changing pressure.

Handling Fish

A landing net is necessary for landing large fish or fish that have very hard or very soft jaws. A gaff is better for big fish that are difficult to get into a net.

When a landing net is not being used, fish without dangerous teeth can be handled by inserting the thumb into the mouth and grasping the lower jaw beween thumb and forefinger. The fish is lifted in this manner and its mouth can be opened by downward pressure to remove the hook. Large fish can be killed immediately by hitting them behind the head with a small club kept for the purpose.

Fish with sharp teeth can be grasped behind the eyes on the gill covers, with the thumb on one side and the forefinger on the other side of the head.

Fish Care

Fish are frequently mishandled after they are caught, so that by the time the fisherman is ready to eat them, they may not be worth eating. As soon as they are caught they should be put on a stringer through the soft skin covering the lower jaw. Stringing fish through the gills is not only unnecessary but painful, and the fish die from it. A live-well is best.

Fish that cannot tolerate warm water should not be kept on a stringer if the surface water is too warm for them because they might die and spoil before they are ready to clean. A better way is to have an ice chest as standard equipment and to put the fish in it as soon as they are caught. Trout and salmon are two kinds of fish that spoil easily.

Very large fish or fish with weak underjaws should not be placed on stringers because they might break loose.

Fish that are to be released should not be allowed to come in contact with dirt, rough surfaces, or dry hands. Any contact will scrape off the protective mucous and permit fungus infections to develop. These infections cause a slow death.

Fishing Manners

- It has been a long standing tradition that a fisherman should be left undisturbed, whether he is on a lake, river, or stream. This is not always possible as the population increases and fishing pressure increases along with it. But if the tradition breaks down, so will the quality of fishing. Avoid getting too close.
- One fisherman should not move around another to get upstream because that is the direction the second man will be going. The exception would be when a run is occurring and everyone is packed into the available space.
- Litter has been a problem for many years and in some places it has hurt the fishing by disturbing breeding areas along the shoreline.
- Fishing line should only be discarded in a closed container. Birds attempt to use it as nesting material and get tangled in it, causing death or serious injury.
- Cans and can tabs frequently get caught on small animals' heads and legs, causing suffering and death. Always discard them in a proper place.

9

Fish and Fishing Methods

This section provides information about most species of fresh water fish of interest to the fisherman. Techniques for catching fish that are included can usually be applied to catching similar species that are not.

Identification of fish is sometimes difficult because of the confusing nature of local and common names for them. Fish families frequently have misnamed members, and a member of the *Perch Family*, the *Walleye*, is often called a *Walleyed Pike*. The only true members of the fresh water Basses are the *White Bass*, the *Yellow Bass*, and the *White Perch*. All other basses are members of the *Sunfish Family*, so to make identification positive, the scientific names have been included with the common names.

Fish identification is simplified by first matching the shape of the fish to a fish family, then by matching the markings of the fish to the key drawings. Color matching should be the last step, based on the color descriptions included with each fish. Colors can be deceptive because variations may occur from one region to another, from one season to another, or when the fish is exposed to air for more than a few minutes.

Descriptions of Fish Families

Bass Family

The dorsal (back) fins are distinctly separated. Bodies are compact. The front dorsal has strong spines, but the rear dorsal is spineless.

Catfish Family

Each member has eight very sensitive barbels (whiskers) used for finding food. All members are scaleless and have sharp spines in the dorsal (back) fins and pectoral (lower front) fins that can cause painful puncture wounds. Most of the 30 species of catfishes are found in muddy water, but the sportiest, the *Channel Catfish*, is found in clear, fast moving water. The largest is the *Blue Catfish*, which may weigh 150 pounds or more. A small species, the *Brindled Madtom*, is only 3 or 4 inches long.

Perch Family

Bodies are slim and elongated. Dorsal fins are distinctly separated. Members are not strong fighters, but are excellent food fish with firm, flaky, white meat.

Pike Family

Bodies are long and slim, with single, spineless dorsal (back) fins that are located near the tails. Their jaws are long and narrow with sharp teeth. Members of the *Pike Family* are fierce fighters, and large ones can be dangerous when they are landed.

Salmon and Trout Family

Bodies are of medium proportions with large dorsal fins located in the centers of the backs, and small adipose (fatty) fins near the tails. Scales are small. Although some species are better eating than others, all are good to excellent food fishes.

They are highly prized as game fishes because of their wariness and fighting nature.

Sunfish Family

All sunfishes are somewhat chunky, and have short bodies with distinctive dorsal fins. The spiny forward section of the dorsal is connected to a soft, flexible rear section. Most species are strong fighters and most are good eating. The best food fish among them is probably the *Bluegill*. Sunfishes are widespread, plentiful, and include more than 30 species.

BASS FAMILY

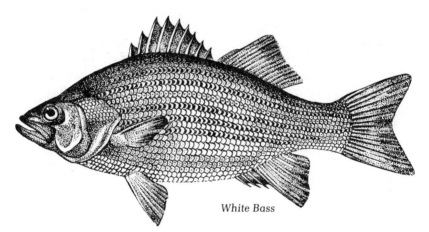

White Bass

White Bass   *Morone chrysops*

Common maximum weight: 1½ lbs./North American record: weight: 5 lbs. 5 oz./length: 19½ in./place: California/year: 1972.

Description

The body is deep and stubby, silvery in color, tinged with gold along the lower sides. The dorsal fins are distinctly separated. The sides have narrow, longitudinal lines extending from head to tail.

63

Range

South central Canada, through Great Lakes to New York. Mississippi River system, Missouri River system, most southern states, west to Texas. Introduced elsewhere.

Character

White bass are basically open water fish that move in schools and range widely both day and night, foraging for small fish. They hit lures hard and quickly.

Location

In the spring, white bass make spawning runs upstream in rivers and streams. They are easily caught at that time. During the summer months, white bass may be anywhere at any time in large lakes and rivers, but like most other fish, they head for deep water on warm, sunny days. They may move into the shallows toward evening as the water surface cools. They have a preference for still water over sand, gravel, or hard clay, near breaklines.

Season

Spring through fall

Time

White bass can be caught both day and night, but early morning and late afternoon are the best times for surface fishing because the surface is usually smooth, and the water temperature is right.

Water Temperature Activity Range

58°–64° F.

Food

Bait fish such as emerald shiners, gizzard shad, some crustaceans, worms, and insects

64

Tackle

BAITCASTING: Ultralight with 4 to 8 pound test line and 1/8 to 1/4 ounce lures.
SPINCAST: Light or medium with 4 to 8 pound test monofilament line and 1/8 to 1/4 ounce lures.
SPINNING: Light or medium with 4 to 8 pound test monofilament line and 1/8 to 1/4 ounce lures.
FLYCASTING: 7½ to 8½ foot rod with No. 5 or No. 6 line.
HOOK SIZES: No. 6 to No. 10.

Lures

Jigs in white, red, yellow, or combinations of these colors. Wobbling spoons, spinners, streamers, plugs in silver, gold, yellow, white, or shad colors.

Baits

Minnows, gizzard shad, crayfish

Methods

Surface actions of bait fish may indicate white bass in pursuit early in the morning and late in the afternoon on calm water. Since white bass travel in schools, action may be fast, so it is necessary to be prepared.

The boat should not intrude on the schools, but be in position so that lures can be cast into them from the edges. Lures should usually be retrieved rapidly to imitate escaping bait fish.

Two jigs on a 3-way swivel, attached with leaders of 15 inches and 7 inches, can be cast into a surface school with excellent results. Both jigs are hit frequently.

Larger white bass can often be taken by casting diving lures over a school and retrieving them from 8 to 10 feet under the surface.

If schools cannot be seen on the surface, trolling with a spoon, spinner, or diving plug is an effective method for locating them. The same lures can be cast to locate schools, but casting is much slower, particularly when large areas must be covered.

When a school has been found, lures can be bottom-bumped, or if the boat is anchored in shallow water, the lures can be cast deep, allowed to touch bottom, then retrieved rapidly while alternating the reeling with short pumps of the rod.

Live baits are not recommended for use when the white bass are on the surface chasing prey fish because the actions of both fish and fisherman are too strenuous for bait to remain on the hook in good condition. In addition, fewer fish will be caught while the fisherman is wasting time baiting the hook between casts.

Live baits can be used effectively when a school of white bass is located in deep water. Attach enough weight to get the bait to the bottom, then retrieve rapidly, arcing the bait while alternating reeling with short pumps of the rod.

Similar Species

Yellow Bass (Morone interruptus)

RANGE: Mississippi drainage, south from Minnesota.

CATFISH FAMILY

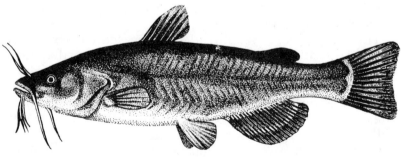

Black Bullhead

Black Bullhead   *Ictalurus melas*

Common maximum weight: 2/3 lb./North American record: weight: 8 lbs./length: 24 in./place: New York/year: 1951

66

Description

The body is scaleless, of medium proportions, with a dark back and belly. The mouth and head are wide with eight barbels (whiskers) used for locating food. The dorsal and pectoral fins have sharp spines on the front edges.

Range

One or more of the three species are found from Maine to the Dakotas, south to Texas and Florida. Introduced to the West Coast.

Character

Bullheads spawn in spring. The eggs are laid in a nest and are guarded by the male which continues to guard the newly hatched young until they are large enough to take care of themselves. Bullheads are tough and can survive on a variety of plant and animal food. They sometimes gather in large groups for feeding.

Location

Bullheads are commonly found in ponds, streams, and lakes with muddy bottoms.

Season

They are caught from spring to fall, but early in the season is usually best.

Time

Bullheads are mainly night feeders, but will bite during the day. Early evening is a good time to begin fishing.

Water Temperature Activity Range

67°–85° F.

Food

Varied diet of vegetation, carrion, crayfish, insect larva, snails, insects, crustaceans

Tackle

SPINCAST: Light with 4 to 8 pound test line.
SPINNING: Ultralight or light with 2 to 6 pound test line.
FLYCASTING: 6 to 7½ foot rod with No. 4 or No. 5 line.
HOOK SIZES: No. 4 to No. 6.

Lures

Plastic worms dressed with a piece of crayfish tail, fish, or entrails to give it a scent.

Baits

Minnows, worm clusters, nightcrawlers, shrimp, crayfish tails, cut fish, stinkbaits, doughballs, entrails, liver, corn kernels strung on a hook

Methods

The bait should be kept on or near the bottom, motionless. The hook can be set after a couple of nibbles followed by a solid pull. A delay in setting the hook will give the bullhead time to suck it into the stomach.

Similar Species

Brown Bullhead (Ictalurus nebulosus)

Yellow Bullhead (Ictalurus natalis)

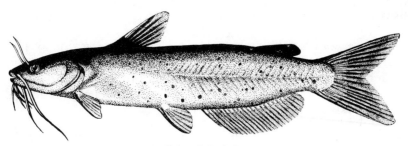

Channel Catfish

Channel Catfish *Ictalurus punctatus*

Common maximum weight: 4½ lbs./North American record: weight: 58 lbs./length: 47½ in./place: South Carolina/year: 1964

Description

The dark body is somewhat slender and covered with small black spots. They are scaleless. The tail is deeply forked. The dorsal and pectoral fins have sharp, protective spines on the front edges. The head has eight, sensitive barbels (whiskers) used to locate food.

Range

South central Canada, west to Montana, east to the St. Lawrence River. Rivers of the Great Lakes region and Mississippi drainage, flowing to the Gulf of Mexico. Delaware River in the east, Snake River in the west.

Character

Channel catfish are the most active members of the catfish family, and prefer moving water, clean and cool.

Location

Channel catfish are located in clear, fast streams and rivers, sometimes in lakes. In rivers they stay near fallen trees, undercut banks, over bars, in protected holes and below dams behind the abutments. In lakes they prefer narrows between lakes or islands.

Season

Spring through fall (They become inactive at less than 50 degrees.)

Time

Night is the best time to fish for channel catfish. They may feed at any depth, sometimes close to the surface.

Water Temperature Activity Range

60°–75° F.

Food

Clams, aquatic insects and larvae, crustaceans, crayfish

Tackle

BAITCASTING: Light or medium with 6 to 15 pound test line.
SPINCAST: Light or medium with 6 to 15 pound test line.
SPINNING: Medium with 6 to 10 pound test line.
FLYCASTING: 8½ to 9½ foot rod with No. 8 to No. 10 line.
HOOK SIZES: No. 4 to No. 2/0. Local fish sizes determine selection.

Lures

Plastic worms, or piece of sponge (½" x ½" x 1") soaked in scent.

Bait

Crayfish, catalpa worms, entrails, dead minnows, smelly cheese mixed with mashed fish or dough, chicken liver, shrimp, red worms cluster, nightcrawlers.

Methods

A productive catfish rig is a bobber, heavy sinker, and a scented bait. The bait is cast upstream into a deep channel and allowed to drift downstream. The bobber can be adjusted to different depths if one depth does not get results.

Another method is to bottom fish with a slip-sinker. A swivel is placed below the slip-sinker on the line, and a monofilament leader about 18 inches long is tied to the swivel. The hook is tied on to the leader end and baited. Once on the bottom, the bait is given free movement through the sinker for several feet. Then if a fish takes the bait, the sinker will not hold it back. If a sponge lure is used, it should be re-scented after each hit by a fish or after it has been in the water for more than five minutes.

PERCH FAMILY

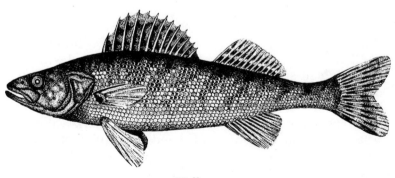

Walleye

Walleye *Stizostedion vitreum*

Common maximum weight: 3½ lbs./North American record: weight: 25 lbs./length: 41 in./place: Tennessee/year: 1960

Description

The body is slim and elongated. The sides and back are brassy yellow and gold with olive green and yellow mottling. The belly is white. The dorsal fins are distinctly separated with a spiny front fin and a soft, flexible rear fin. The eyes are milky in appearance. They are excellent food fish.

Range

Central and eastern Canada, south to northern Alabama, northern Arkansas, west to Nebraska.

Character

Walleyes travel in loose schools, and are on the move much of the time. They make spawning runs up rivers when possible, sometimes for a great many miles. Spawning is done in spring, in moving water with sand or gravel bottom. They are strong, fast swimmers, but not always strong fighters.

Location

Walleyes are found in rivers and lakes of different types. They do best in moderately fertile waters, but can be found in bog lakes, clear, soft water lakes, and fertile hardwater lakes.

In summer during the day, lake walleyes usually remain near drop-offs and bars in deep water from 15 to 50 feet deep.

In lakes of less than 30 feet in depth with dark water, they may be located at the edges of weed beds on more gradual slopes at depths of only 5 to 7 feet. Deep or shallow, walleyes avoid direct sunlight and seek out well-shaded areas.

Walleyes move into shallower water at sunset near rocks, bars, and ridges where the bottom is covered with sand or gravel. They move out again at dawn after feeding all night.

In the hottest weather they may remain in deep water at night and continue to feed there even though more food could be found in shallow water.

In the spring and fall, walleyes move into the shallow areas during the day when the water is cool, but in winter, they remain in deep water where they feed actively. They may be found in shallow water on cloudy days or when the water is turbid during summer.

Season

Walleyes are active all year.

Time

Walleyes feed most actively at night, but they can be caught during the day on cloudy days, in turbid water, or in deep, shaded places.

Water Temperature Activity Range

54°–70° F.

Food

Small fish, crayfish, larger aquatic insects, leeches

Tackle

BAITCASTING: Light with 6 to 10 pound test line and 1/4 to 1/2 ounce lures.
SPINCAST: Light with 4 to 10 pound test line and 1/8 to 3/8 ounce lures.
SPINNING: Light or medium with 4 to 10 pound test line and 1/8 to 3/8 ounce lures.
FLYCASTING: 7½ to 8½ foot rod with No. 6 or No. 7 line.
HOOK SIZES: No. 4 to No. 8.

Lures

Deep-diving plugs, weighted spinners with pork rind dressings, wobbling spoons with pork rind, minnow imitations, marabou jigs, jigs with soft plastic bodies, streamers, poppers for surface fishing. Colors in yellow, purple, black, and combinations.

Baits

Minnows, crayfish, night crawlers, and leeches

Methods

Walleyes can be located on lakes by trolling with a weighted, floating lure, nightcrawler, minnow, crayfish, or large leech. An effective trolling rig is a 3-way swivel, 10–20 inches of leader from swivel to hook, and about 18 inches of leader from the swivel to a dipsey sinker.

Backtrolling (see page 55) is also a good method for locating walleyes. A bottom-walking, slip-sinker rig is very effective with a large leech hooked behind a twister plastic lure. The leeches are extremely tough and will not be lost as easily as nightcrawlers. There should be no drag on the line so that the fish can carry the bait without resistance.

Walleyes sometimes stop hitting after three or four fish have been caught. If that occurs, the bait or lure should be changed from one type to another as often as necessary.

When a slip-sinker rig is used from a set position, the rod is twitched every 30 seconds or so to add action to the bait. If no hits result, the bait can be retrieved a few feet and then given a free line again. Repeat the process.

Spinning or spincast tackle rigged with a jig or jig head and a nightcrawler or jumbo leech may produce when other lures or baits won't. The rod is held at shoulder height and the jig is lifted off the bottom very slightly, allowed to drop, then lifted. The bottom is touched lightly and actual jigging should be avoided.

Live bait is usually effective for still fishing, but for casting over weeds and bars, a sinking lure works well, especially if the lure is dressed with a minnow, nightcrawler, leech or pork rind. Bottom bumping improves the chances for catching walleyes in deep water.

Night fishing for walleyes requires preparation. Breaklines and bottom structure should be studied thoroughly during daylight hours so that time is not wasted during the fishing period.

Similar Species

Sauger (Stizostedion canadense)

RANGE: Similar to walleye.

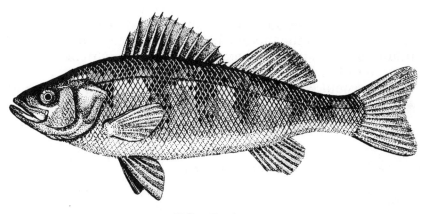

Yellow Perch

Yellow Perch   *Perca flavescens*

Common maximum weight: 1/2 lb./North American record: weight: 4 lbs. 3 oz./place: New Jersey/year: 1865

Description

The body is elongated with greenish to golden yellow sides and back. Bands of dark color extend from the back to about halfway down the sides. The belly is white to yellowish. They are excellent as food fish.

Range

Eastern and central Canada, south to South Carolina, Ohio, and Kansas. Stocked elsewhere.

Character

Yellow perch of similar size school in groups and migrate daily from open water to a resting bar where they remain until sunset when they return to open water.

Location

In early spring, perch spawn in shallow water, sometimes migrating up streams when they are available.

During the day in warm weather, they may be found in the upper part of the thermocline, in bays, near sand bars, and around piers. In hot weather, perch may remain in deep water from 20 to 70 feet.

After cold weather sets in, the perch move to deep water where they remain if the oxygen supply is sufficient.

Season

Yellow perch are active all year.

Time

The best times to catch perch are from about 10:00 a.m. to 2:00 p.m. and from 4:00 p.m. to 6:00 p.m.

Water Temperature Activity Range

60°–75° F.

Food

Insects, crayfish, small fish, worms, insect larvae, crustaceans

Tackle

SPINCAST: Light with 4 to 8 pound test line with 1/8 to 1/4 ounce lures.
SPINNING: Ultralight with 2 to 4 pound test line and 1/16 to 1/4 ounce lures.
FLYCASTING: 6 to 7½ foot rod with No. 4 or No. 5 line.
HOOK SIZES: No. 6 to No. 8.

Lures

Small to medium-sized wobbling spoons, spinners, jigs, flies

Baits

Worms, small minnows, minnow-spinner combinations, crickets, grasshoppers, mealworms, flies, shrimp pieces, fish pieces, crayfish tails, grubs

Methods

Schools of perch can be located by trolling or drifting a weighted fly or a minnow behind a small spinner. Drift casting is another method. The bait is allowed to sink to the weed tops before it is retrieved. Minnows, flies, and weedless spoons can be used for casting.

A third method is to use a bobber, and float the bait over the weeds using split-shot for weight. Split-shot provide sufficient weight to control the bait without holding it down. If a minnow is used under a bobber, the hook is set after the perch runs with it and stops. With other baits, set the hook quickly. After the school is located, the bobber can be removed for better rod action and depth control.

Since perch school according to size, the boat can be anchored after fish of respectable size have been located. When the depth of the perch has been determined, the lures or baits can be cast to the proper depth or still-fished.

PIKE FAMILY

Muskellunge

Muskellunge   *Esox masquinongy*

Common maximum weight: 15 lbs./common maximum length: 45 in./North American record: weight: 69 lbs. 15 oz./ length: 64½ in./place: New York/year: 1957

Description

The body is long and slim. The single dorsal fin is spineless and located near the tail. Both the cheek and gill covers are scaled on the upper halves, but are unscaled on the lower sections. The jaws are long, hard, and narrow with sharp teeth. *Esox masquinongy* has dark spots over a silver-gray background. *Esox masquinongy ohiensis* (Chautauqua Muskellunge) has dark vertical stripes on a light yellow-green background. *Esox masquinongy immaculatus* (Northern Muskellunge) has dark vertical stripes over a light gray-green background. The back, tail, and fins are reddish in color.

Range

Southern Canada, through the Great Lakes region and upper Mississippi drainage.

Character

Muskellunge are loners that stay almost motionless, concealed in vegetation in quiet water .They are difficult to catch because of their temperament and hard mouths, but when they strike they lunge from cover to hit the lure with force. They are sight feeders, curious and bold.

Location

Muskellunge are found in clear water in lakes, rivers, and flowages. They stay close to vegetation near channels, in bays, near sand bars, ledges, logs, drop-offs, and over-hanging trees. Usually they are located in less than 15 feet of water, but may go as deep as 50 feet on occasion.

In spring and fall, muskellunge can be found in shallow water, but during the summer they go deeper to find cool water. In lakes with limited cisco or whitefish populations, but good populations of walleyes, muskies follow schools of small walleyes and feed on them throughout the year.

Season

Spring to fall

Time

Daylight hours

Water Temperature Activity Range

60°–75° F.

Food

Crayfish, fish, small mammals, young water birds

Tackle

BAITCASTING: Heavy or ultraheavy with 20 to 40 pound test line and 1 to 2 ounce lures or more.
HOOK SIZES: 2/0 to 5/0. Single hooks preferred over treble by some fishermen. Wire or very heavy monofilament leaders are necessary, testing between 60 and 75 pounds.

Lures

Spinners, wobbling spoons, shallow-diving plugs, active spoons with a large bucktail in rear, deep-diving plugs, jigs

Baits

Suckers, 10 inches or more in length. They should be harnessed for most conditions, particularly for casting.

Methods

Plugs, spoons, and other lures can be trolled along the edges of weed beds. It is sometimes effective to use a live bait under a bobber and troll very slowly, or drift the bait.

Weed edges can be fan-cast, but snags are to be avoided because dislodging them frightens the fish. Retrievals should be fast, in imitation of a wounded fish. Sometimes a musky will follow a lure but not strike. Each cast should be followed by a few figure 8 movements near the boat to encourage a response.

When a musky strikes, the hook must be set quickly and solidly. The line must be kept taut at all times, and the fish should be kept away from the boat by circling with it until it is tired. Early signs of tiring cannot always be believed.

A net or gaff is necessary to land a muskellunge, but a gaff makes it necessary to keep the fish. If a net is used, the fish should be led into it head first. If the musky is going to be kept, it should be grasped behind the head on the gill covers, held down, and struck over the head with a club to kill it. Care must be taken to avoid injuring the musky because a wounded muskellunge can do considerable damage to a boat or one's fingers, arms and legs. (See TROLLING, pp. 54-57.)

Sub-Species

Northern Muskellunge (Tiger Muskellunge) (Esox masquinongy immaculatus)

RANGE: Limited to Minnesota and Wisconsin.

Chautauqua Muskellunge (Esox masquinongy ohiensis)

RANGE: In some lakes from the St. Lawrence River to the Ohio River system.

Northern Pike

Northern Pike   *Esox lucius*

Common maximum weight: 8 lbs./North American record: weight: 46 lbs. 2 oz./length: 52½ in./place: New York/year: 1940

Description

The body is long and slim with the single, spineless, dorsal fin located near the tail. The body color is basically dark, blue-gray and green-gray, with a purplish luster over the back and sides. The color lightens to yellowish toward the belly where it becomes white. The sides are covered with irregular rows of small, light yellowish spots. The entire cheek is covered with scales, but only the upper half of the gill cover. The jaws are long, hard, and narrow with sharp teeth.

Range

Arctic Circle, south through Canada to North Carolina, west to Missouri, Colorado, and Montana.

Character

Northern pike may congregate in loose groups during spawning season, then they gradually disperse and become solitary. At that time, they can be caught in numbers within a limited area, but not during active spawning.

Northerns hunt by sight and rush from cover to attack their prey.

Location

During spawning season they can be found in streams, shallow bays, and coves. As long as the water is cool, they will stay in shallow water with some cover near bars. As the water warms, the pike go into deeper water near vegetation, usually under 15 feet. Larger northerns may be found in water from 25 to 40 feet deep in summer near bars and drop-offs. They also stay around spring inlets where the water is cold.

Season

Spring and fall are best, but they can be caught all year.

Time

Daylight hours, early in morning, early evening, or on overcast days.

Water Temperature Activity Range

60°–75° F.

Food

Fish such as perch and suckers, some crayfish

Tackle

BAITCASTING: Medium or heavy with 10 to 25 pound test line, and 3/4 ounce lures or more.
SPINCAST: Heavy with 10 to 15 pound test line, and 1/2 to 5/8 ounce lures.
SPINNING: Heavy with 10 to 15 pound test line, and 5/8 to 1½ ounce lures.
FLYCASTING: 9 to 9½ foot rod with No. 9 or No. 10 line with a short leader.
HOOK SIZES: 1/0 to 3/0 with wire leaders. Single hooks preferred over treble by some fishermen. Monofilament shock leaders may be used in place of wire leaders.

Lures

Fish imitations, long spoons in silver shades or red and white combinations with bucktail or pork rind strips added. Medium-sized plugs, weedless pork frogs, streamers, jigs with a 3 or 4 inch minnow added.

Baits

Small suckers, large shiners, small perch, or chubs from 3 to 8 inches. Smaller ones can be hooked through the lips or under the dorsal fin and used as dressing on jigs. Crayfish hooked through the tail.

Methods

After spawning in the spring, pike can be caught by fishing with a jig-minnow combination along bars with some weed cover. Long sweeps are made with the jig, moving it quite rapidly but touching bottom at the end of a sweep. This provides a continuous guide to the bar location and water depth.

Another method for locating pike in spring is by trolling with a spoon. Fishing can be continued after they have been found by casting the lure and retrieving it in imitation of a wounded fish. This is accomplished with spurts of speed alternated with rest periods or with a jigging action. If surface lures are used, this method should only be used when the northerns are in shallow water.

In cold water with live bait, the hook should not be set until the fish has made a run with it for a short distance and stopped for a few minutes. Baits are usually carried off for several feet before being swallowed.

As the water surface begins to warm and vegetation begins to grow, a slip-sinker rig with a 3 to 6 inch minnow will get better results until cool fall weather moves in. At this time a spinner and a 2 to 4 inch shiner minnow, in combination, is more productive. In fall when the weeds are fully developed and the water begins to cool, another method is to drift a large minnow under a bobber over weed beds. Lures cast or trolled parallel to the weed edges also work well. Lures should be fished at several depths, from shallow to deep.

In late fall when northerns return to the shallows, they can be caught on surface lures, spoons, or spinners retrieved at fairly high speeds.

Like the muskellunge, the northern pike can be deceptive when hooked. It may seem to be completely exhausted, but once it is near the boat, it may suddenly explode with power and break loose. A landing net or gaff is necessary to land it, and if a net is used, the fish should be led into it head first. (See TROLLING, pp. 54-57.)

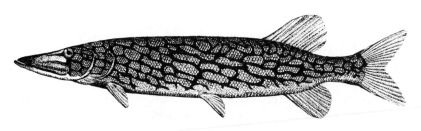

Chain Pickerel

Chain Pickerel *Esox niger*

Common maximum weight: 2½ lbs./North American record: weight: 9 lbs. 6 oz./length: 31 in./place: Georgia/year: 1961

Description

The body is long and slim with a single, spineless dorsal fin located near the tail. The cheek and gill covers are entirely covered with scales. Body color is basically gold-yellow, dark on the back gradually changing to light with the belly almost white. An overlay of a bold, greenish-black mesh pattern provides the chain pickerel with a distinct pattern. The patterns of *Esox vermiculatus* (Grass Pickerel) and *Esox americanus* (Redfin Pickerel) are irregular vertical bands.

Range

Chain pickerel are found in lakes and streams along the Atlantic Coast from Canada to Florida, west to Texas.

Character

Pickerel are solitary, very aggressive fish that feed during the day by sight. They strike with great force, hitting the prey when it comes within range of the pickerel's hiding place.

Location

Pickerel are found in shallow water with sandy or muddy bottoms, among eel grass and other vegetation, or around logs, brush, or trees. They usually do not extend their movements beyond 8 feet of water or so. They face away from shore, but if the shallows nearest the shore do not provide sufficient cover, pickerel will be in off-shore weed beds facing toward shore. Sloughs and side-channels are attractive to pickerel in rivers or impoundments because of the vegetation and slow-moving water.

Season

Pickerel are active all year, but cool or cold weather is best.

Time

Daylight hours. Overcast days are more productive, particularly on large lakes and rivers.

Water Temperature Activity Range

60°–75° F.

Food

Minnows, small fish, frogs

Tackle

BAITCASTING: Ultralight or light with 4 to 10 pound test line and 1/4 to 1/2 ounce lures.
SPINCAST: Light or medium with 4 to 10 pound test line and 1/4 to 1/2 ounce lures.
SPINNING: Light or medium with 4 to 10 pound test line and 1/4 to 5/8 ounce lures.
FLYCASTING: 8 to 9 foot rod with No. 6 or No. 7 line.
HOOK SIZES: 2 to 2/0 long shank, with 10 pound monofilament leader.

Lures

Small fish imitations in spoons, streamers, plugs. Frog imitations, pork rind additions on spoons. Colors in red, greens, yellows, silver.

Baits

Minnows, cut bait, pork rind

Methods

Casts made parallel to the edges of weed beds can get excellent results. The casts should begin short and be gradually lengthened until an area is thoroughly covered. Lures should be retrieved at a fairly rapid rate with variations in movements. They are supposed to imitate live prey that may be injured.

"Skittering" is a popular method for catching pickerel, using a long, stiff pole usually cane. A line about the same length as the pole, is used with a pork rind frog as bait. The bait is swung out over the weed beds as the boat moves slowly past them. Then it is pulled back across the surface, either in a continuous smooth action or in short, uneven jerks.

Similar Species

Grass Pickerel (Esox vermiculatus)

RANGE: Maine to Florida in the east, west to Minnesota.

Redfin Pickerel (Esox americanus)

RANGE: East coast states.

SALMON AND TROUT FAMILY

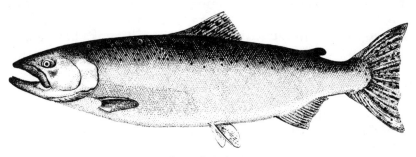

Chinook Salmon

Chinook or King Salmon   *Oncorhynchus tshawytscha*

Common maximum weight: 22 lbs.—Lake Michigan/33 lbs.—Pacific coast/North American record (fresh water): weight: 42 lbs./place: Michigan/year: 1970/North American record (salt water): weight: 93 lbs./length: 50 in./place: Alaska/year: 1977

Description

The body is of medium proportions, but filled out well. The blue-green back color changes to light gold, then to silver-white down the sides and on the belly. The back dorsal fin and tail are covered with small, dark spots. The scales are small. The dorsal fin is located in the center of the back with a small adipose (fatty) fin near the tail. Colors vary with sex, season, and age.

Range

Coastal bays and rivers from California to Alaska. Successfully introduced to the Great Lakes, but do not reproduce because of the effects of water pollution on the spawn in the home rivers, or because of obstacles.

Character

Chinook salmon travel in schools, which break up in hot weather, as they move toward deep, cool water. Around spawning time, from late summer to early winter, the salmon congregate within their home regions in the Great Lakes before migrating up their rivers to spawn. Chinooks have a four-year spawning cycle.

Location

Movements in the Great Lakes and elsewhere are determined by food supply, water temperature, weather, and other factors.

In Lake Michigan, salmon are found on the southern end of the lake after the ice breaks up at the end of March or early April. As the water warms, they begin moving along both sides of the lake and can be found near river mouths or within a mile from shore.

Warm weather drives the salmon into deep water from ten to twenty miles off shore.

Approximate movements of salmon on the Michigan side of Lake Michigan are listed below. Movements on the Wisconsin side occur about two weeks later.

April to May 15	lower 1/4 of the lake
May 15 to August 1	second 1/4 of the lake
August 1 to October 1	third 1/4 of the lake
October 1 through November	upper 1/4 of the lake

By late summer, cohos and chinooks are re-schooling within their home regions for the fall spawning runs up their home rivers. By mid-September, the river migrations are well under way, lasting through November in the north end of the lake.

When they are re-schooling to migrate upstream, salmon can be found near river mouths, in bays, near breakwaters and piers, or in concentrations further out in the lake. Their movements are closely connected with the movements of alewives. Local conditions should be checked daily.

Season

Early spring to late fall in the Great Lakes. Late fall is best.

Time

Sunny, bright days should be avoided. Surface fishing for salmon is best early in the morning, but late in the day after sundown is also good. Deep fishing near the thermocline can be productive at any time of the day.

Water Temperature Activity Range

50°–60° F.

Food

Alewives, smelt

Tackle

DEEP TROLLING: Heavy action, two-handed trolling rod with roller guides or tungsten carboloy guides with a roller tip. Large capacity, level-wind reel, holding up to 200 yards of 20 to 30 pound test metal line.

BOAT AND PIER: Long, medium to heavy action, two-handed rod, with large capacity, level-wind reel, holding up to 200 yards of 12 to 25 pound test monofilament line, with 5/8 to 1½ ounce lures.

SPINNING: Ultraheavy action rod, with large capacity reel, 15 to 20 pound test monofilament line and 5/8 to 1½ ounce lures. Used with a 7 foot, 10 to 12 pound test monofilament leader.

FLYCASTING: 9 to 9½ foot rod with No. 10 or No. 11 line.

HOOK SIZES: Variable because of variable fish sizes, but 2/0 to 6/0 is a useable range.

Lures

Single hook fluorescent spoons in combinations of red and yellow, yellow and green, green and black, yellow and black, red and black, or variations of silver, gold, or other metallic colors. Plugs and spinners are also good.

Baits

Alewives, smelt, large shiners, suckers

Methods

Surface fishing can be done from piers, bridges, break-waters, and boats. Lures can be cast into schools of salmon and retrieved slowly with variations in the action. If one lure is not productive, another should be tried.

Setting the hook is not necessary and should be avoided. An increase in line pressure is enough to hook the fish. Heavy drag may cause the fish to break loose, but steady line pressure will tire the fish sufficiently for it to be landed.

Slow, shallow trolling in bays, near breakwaters, and near river mouths can also be productive.

Deep still-fishing in 30 to 100 feet or more of water can be accomplished with live bait, cut bait, or a spoon jigged slowly, or fished from a slowly moving boat. Live or cut baits are rigged to tandem hooks about 3 inches apart on the end of a 7 foot leader. The other end of the leader is tied to a swivel and the swivel is attached to a 2 or 3 ounce keel sinker. The sinker is attached to the line. The hooks are placed through the lips and under the dorsal fin of the bait fish. Rigged in this manner, the bait fish can move freely without twisting the line. Care must be taken not to puncture the skulls with the hooks.

Spoons are the basic lures in deep trolling for salmon. The speed of the troll may vary with the lure, so it is important to test the lure at various speeds to get the most natural action. Depth is controlled by adding weights. (see DEEP TROLLING, page 57, 58.)

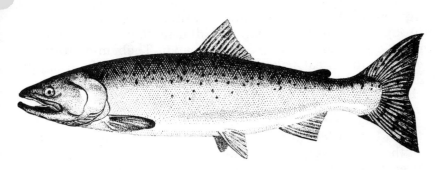

Coho Salmon

Coho or Silver Salmon   *Oncorhynchus kisutch*

Common maximum weight: 9 lbs.-Lake Michigan/12 lbs.-Pacific coast/North American record (fresh water): weight: 27 lbs. 12 oz./place: Michigan/year: 1970/North American record (salt water): weight: 31 lbs./place: British Columbia/year: 1947

Description

The body is of medium proportions. The scales are small. The blue-green back is covered with small, dark spots, but the dorsal fin and tail are not entirely covered. The tail color is darker and bluer than that of the chinook. Body color changes from bluish-gray-green on the back to silver-white on the sides and belly. The dorsal fin is in the center of the back with a small adipose (fatty) fin near the tail. During the spawning season the males turn red.

Range

Coastal bays and rivers from California to Alaska. Successfully introduced to the Great Lakes, but do not reproduce because of the effects of water pollution on spawn or because of obstacles.

Character

Coho salmon are school fish which break up in summer as

91

they move toward deep, cool water. From late summer through fall, they re-school, and after three years of maturing, migrate up their home rivers to spawn. Their migratory patterns on the Great Lakes are determined by the food supply and other factors, such as water temperature and weather.

Location

In Lake Michigan, cohos and chinooks can be found at the southern end beginning at the end of March or early April. After the ice breaks up, they begin moving up both sides of the lake. At that time fishing is good near river mouths and bays or within a mile of the shore. By mid-June they may be 10 to 20 miles out in the lake to find cool water. (see Chinook *Location*, pages 88, 89.)

Season

Early spring to late fall

Time

Surface fishing can be productive near shore early in the morning or after sundown. During the day, cohos are found in deep water near the thermocline, except on overcast days when they may remain near the shore.

Water Temperature Activity Range

45°–60° F.

Food

Alewives, smelt

Tackle

DEEP TROLLING: Heavy action, two-handed trolling rod, with roller guides, or tungsten carboloy guides with a roller tip. Large capacity, level-wind reel, holding up to 200 yards of 20 to 30 pound test metal line.
BOAT AND PIER: Long, medium action, two-handed rod, with large capacity, level-wind reel holding up to 200 yards of 10 to 15 pound test monofilament line and 5/8 to 1 ounce lures.

Used with 7 foot leader, 6 to 8 pound test, for better action and less visibility.

SPINNING: Medium to heavy action rod with large capacity reel, 8 to 15 pound test monofilament line, and 1/2 to 3/4 ounce lures. Used with 7 foot, 6 to 8 pound test monofilament leader.

FLYCASTING: 8½ to 9½ foot rod with No. 9 to No. 11 line.

HOOK SIZES: No. 1 to No. 3/0. Sizes variable because of varying fish sizes.

Lures

Single hook, fluorescent spoons in combinations of red-yellow, yellow-green, gold-green, yellow-black, red-black, and metallic colors. Spinners, plugs, cowbells, streamers.

Baits

Alewives, smelt, salmon eggs, whole fresh shrimp

Methods

(See Chinook Salmon, pages 87-90.) When salmon are schooling on the surface, near rivers, or in bays, they can be fished from piers, bridges, breakwaters, and boats.

Live bait, cut bait, or spoons can be jigged in deep water, and spoons in particular can be trolled effectively. (see DEEP TROLLING, pages 57, 58.)

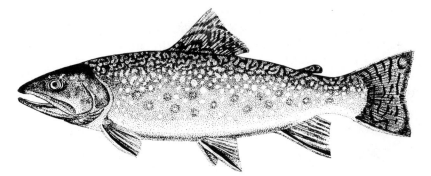

Brook Trout

Brook Trout   *Salvelinus fontinalis*

Common maximum weight: 1½ lbs./North American record: weight: 14 lbs. 8 oz./length: 31½ in./place: Ontario/year: 1916

Description

The body is of medium proportions. The body color ranges from mottled bluish-black on the back to yellow-green on the middle of both sides. The red spots may be surrounded by blue. The dorsal fin is in the center of the back with a small adipose (fatty) fin near the tail. The front edges of the orange-pink lower fins are edged in white. The scales are small.

Range

Eastern Canada, New England states, west to Minnesota. Introduced to the northwest.

Character

Brook trout are sensitive to low oxygen levels, to water temperature changes, and to any form of pollution. When surface waters are warm, they stay close to the bottom. They may congregate at times, but they do not school. They are easily frightened by movements, shadows, and noises, but are aggressive feeders. They spawn from fall to early winter.

Location

Brook trout inhabit small, cold streams, spring-fed ponds, lakes, and rivers. They are seldom found more than a mile or so from spring water sources in the upper parts of streams. They hide behind rocks, logs, and undercut banks, and congregate in pools near rapids and falls.

Season

Spring to fall

Time

Sunrise and just before sunset are the best times to catch

94

them in streams, but they can also be caught during the day in spring fed lakes in deep water.

Water Temperature Activity Range

47°–63° F.

Food

Small crustaceans, crayfish, nymphs, insect larvae, beetles, ants, grasshoppers, worms, small minnows, seasonal insect hatches

Tackle

SPINNING: Ultralight with 2 to 4 pound test line and 1/16 to 1/8 ounce lures.
FLYCASTING: 6 to 7½ foot rod with No. 4 or No. 5 line.
HOOK SIZES: Wet flies: No. 10 to No. 12. Dry flies: No. 12 to No. 18, or smaller.

Lures

Wet or dry fly imitations of hatching insects in brown, gray, or black. Silver-brass or red-white combinations in spinners, miniature spoons, jigs, streamers, bucktails.

Baits

Nymphs, insect larvae, beetles, grasshoppers, small worms, nightcrawlers

Methods

Wet or dry flies should be matched to seasonal insect hatches, and after a rain, flies can be used that imitate insects that were washed into the water.

When metal lures are used, it is best to match them to light conditions, bright lures on bright days, and so forth.

In small, brush-covered streams, each small opening along the bank can be fished with a worm or insect lowered gently into the water. The line should be kept short to prevent snags, but if an open area can be seen, the bait can be drifted into it. The fisherman must remain out of sight at all times, so neutral clothing should be worn and movements should be very slow.

In open areas, flies or baits can be cast upstream and across, then allowed to drift downstream over riffles and into pools.

One of the best ways to catch brook and other trout is with an imitation of a leaf-roller. This larva is yellow-green in color and 3/4 of an inch long. It is abundant in forests from about mid-May to late June, and trout feed on them in bright sunlight during the day.

Brook trout can be caught in lakes from early morning to early evening. Early or late and on overcast days, flies, small spoons, and spinners, fished shallow, are effective. When the trout are deep, they can be caught by trolling or casting with spoons and spinners, or by jigging with miniature jigs or spoons.

Jigs can also be used for shallow fishing in combination with a plastic bubble. The bubble is attached to the end of the line, and the jig leader is tied at right angles to the line, about 12 to 18 inches above the bubble. The bubble controls the depth of the jig, floating above it.

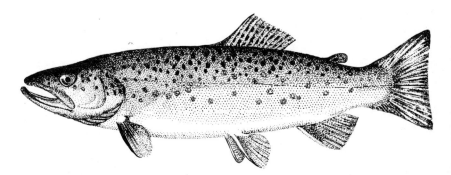

Brown Trout

Brown Trout *Salmontrutta*

Common maximum weight: 2½ lbs./North American record: weight: 32 lbs. 8 oz./length: 34 in./place: Wisconsin (Lake Michigan)/year: 1978

Description

The basic body color is yellow-brown, brownish, or brownish-black, depending upon the local food and water. The body is slightly thicker in appearance than the medium proportions of the rainbow or brook trout. The back is covered with black spots which are mixed with red spots on the sides, some ringed with blue. The dorsal fin has a mixture of black spots and a few red. The dorsal fin is in the center of the back with a small adipose (fatty) fin near the tail. The scales are small.

Brown trout were transplanted from Great Britain in the 1880's. They are now found in clear rivers and lakes of the United States and parts of Canada.

Character

Brown trout are very secretive and difficult to catch because they are super-sensitive to movements. They spawn from October to November in streams with gravel bottoms.

Location

They are found in slow running pools in streams of moderate swiftness with sand and gravel bottoms. They are usually downstream from brook trout, in warmer water and in areas that are more open. They are also common to clean, clear, fairly deep lakes. In the Great Lakes they can be located in sheltered areas, in bays and behind breakwaters.

Season

Spring through fall

Time

The best fishing occurs in the evening, night, and early morning, just before sunrise.

Water Temperature Activity Range

60°–75° F.

Food

Emerging insects, crustaceans, leeches, snails, crayfish (Large trout eat fish also.)

Tackle

SPINNING: Ultralight or light with 2 to 4 pound test line, and 1/16 to 1/4 ounce lures. Medium tackle may be preferred in some regions.
FLYCASTING: 7½ to 8½ foot rod with No. 5 or No. 6 line system.
HOOK SIZES: Wet flies: No. 10 to No. 12. Dry flies: No. 12 to No. 18.

Lures

Small wet or dry flies in imitation of hatching insects, in brown or gray. Bucktails and marabou streamers for larger fish. Spinners, wobbling spoons, and jigs for lake fishing. Midget plugs for large trout. Leaf-roller larva imitation in yellow-green.

Baits

Bait fish of the region, worms, crayfish, hatching insects

Methods

Fishing where heavy brush makes it impossible to cast, or where the stream is too small for casting, can be accomplished by dropping a worm or insect bait on the water and letting it drift downstream as the line is let out. Bait can be made to appear free-floating by using a leader tied at right angles to the line about 12 to 18 inches above a looped end. Split-shot are attached to the loop to hold the line down. The bait follows several inches above the bottom as the split-shot are pushed along by the current. The hook is set when the line twitches.

Where casting is possible, the fly or bait can be cast upstream and given an occasional twitch as it drifts downstream.

In open areas, a side cast and low profile are necessary to prevent being seen, and neutral shades of clothing are equally important.

Insect hatches and seasonal foods should be observed and imitated in appearance and action when flies, nymphs, or insect imitations are used. For example, in late summer, wet flies have an advantage over dry flies because the surface action of the hatches is over. At daybreak, during and after a rain, is the best time for worms and nymphs.

Large river pools of unknown depth can be fished with a weighted bucktail or marabou jigged from the head of the pool.

Brown trout can be caught in large lakes along shorelines, from piers, breakwaters, or from a small boat. Jigs, spoons, and live bait are productive, and spoons or other lures can be trolled.

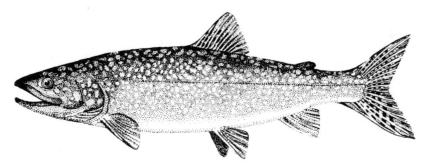

Lake Trout

Lake Trout   *Salvelinus namaycush*

Common maximum weight: 7½ lbs./North American record: weight: 65 lbs./length: 52 in./place: Northwest Territory/year: 1970

Description

The body is of medium proportions and the tail is distinctly forked. The dorsal fin is in the center of the back with a small adipose (fatty) fin near the tail. The scales are small. The basic body color is bluish-gray; it is dark on the back changing to yellowish-gray on the sides and to light gray on the belly. Small, irregular yellow-gray spots cover the back, sides, tail, dorsal, and anal fins.

Range

Alaska to Labrador in the north. Wisconsin to Maine are the southern limits.

Character

Lake trout are deep water fish. They seem to be solitary in their habits, but form loose groupings at times. They migrate to and from the spawning grounds, which may be only a short distance or as much as 200 to 300 miles. They spawn on rocky outcroppings or shoals in 4 to 6 feet of water from late September to the end of November.

Location

Water temperature is crucial to the location of lake trout. They are found in deep lakes with a good oxygen supply and temperature layers. In large lakes, they are located around rocky reefs, in coves with cover, and sand, gravel, or rock bottoms. In spring and fall, they stay nearer the surface, but during the summer, they remain in water from 100 to 300 feet deep where the water is cool. In the far north, lake trout may be near the surface as long as the water remains open. They also follow bait fish levels, up or down.

Season

Lake trout are active all year, but the easiest fishing is in spring on the surface after the ice breaks up, and in the fall after the surface water cools.

Time

Early in the morning, or on cloudy days when the trout are shallow. Deep fishing can be done on any day.

Water Temperature Activity Range

Northern range: 35°–45° F.
Southern range: 40°–55° F.

Food

Alewives, cisco, smelt, perch, whitefish, sculpin and fish common to a specific region (Usually only one or two species are available. Insects are eaten in spring.)

Tackle

DEEP TROLLING: Medium action, two-handed trolling rod, with roller guides, or tungsten carboloy guides with a roller tip. Large capacity, level-wind reel, holding up to 200 yards of 20 to 30 pound test metal line. A single handle reel has better control.
OTHER TROLLING: 7½ to 8 foot, medium action rod, with large level-wind reel with single handle, and 25 pound test monofilament line.
BAITCASTING: Medium to heavy action rod with 10 to 25 pound test line and 5/8 to 1 ounce lures.
SPINCAST: Heavy action with 10 to 15 pound test line and 1/2 to 3/4 ounce lures.
SPINNING: Heavy or ultraheavy action with 12 to 20 pound test line and 5/8 to 1 ounce lures.
HOOK SIZES: 1 to 4/0.

Lures

Large spoons in brass, nickel, copper, pearl. Spinners and spinners in tandem (cowbells), with a minnow or wobbling spoon added. Streamers in white, green, or blue, 4 or 5 inches long. Bucktails and imitations of bait fish. Treble hooks preferred.

Baits

Live or dead bait fish such as herring, sculpin, alewives, minnows, and cut bait (Bait fish of the area should be used.)

Methods

In the spring, lake trout can be located by shallow trolling or casting along the edges of ice floes with minnows, spoons, and other active lures. Weight can be added if necessary. It is common for a lake trout to take a lure as it is sinking.

After water temperatures are checked, an area has been chosen, and proper depth determined, deep trout can be located by trolling with a bait fish or deep running lure behind a cowbell attractor. Proper depth is perhaps more a matter of bait fish location than it is a matter of temperatures preferred by the lake trout. Trolling depths should not be limited to the bottom, but varied for best results. Ideally the lure should run under the bait fish schools where the trout would be. The bait fish feed along shorelines from which the wind is blowing, so chances are much better there.

A 3-way swivel is used for trolling, with a 1½ to 3 ounce weight. The weight is attached with about 2 feet of 6 to 8 pound test leader, and the lure is attached with about 3 feet of line test leader. If a downrigger is not used, a 6 to 8 inch wire leader should precede the cowbells.

Trolling should be done slowly, only fast enough to provide the proper action to the lure. Near the bottom, the weight is bounced every few seconds to check depths and conditions. A slight jigging action while trolling will make the lure more attractive to the trout.

Still fishing can be effective using a heavy, shiny, or luminous spoon. The spoon is lowered to the bottom, then raised 2 or 3 feet and dropped to get a fluttering action .This is repeated. Strikes usually occur while the lure is falling, so the line must be watched carefully while it is slack, and the hook must be set hard.

Another method is to use a live bait fish with a slip-sinker rig. The sinker is attached to the line above a swivel, and 2 or 3 feet of monofilament line is tied to the swivel. The hook and bait fish are attached to the end of the line segment and lowered to the bottom. Several feet of line are released to permit the bait fish to swim about freely within a radius of the sinker. When a trout is felt to be moving away with the bait, the hook is set. (See DEEP TROLLING, pages 57, 58.)

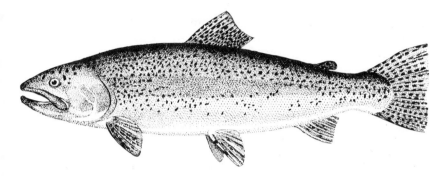

Rainbow and Steelhead Trout

Rainbow and Steelhead Trout *Salmo gairdneri*

Common maximum weight: 2 lbs./length: 18 in./common maximum weight: Great Lakes and Pacific coast: 11 lbs./North American record (fresh water): weight: 37 lbs./place: Idaho/year: 1947/North American record (salt water): weight: 42 lbs. 2 oz./place: Alaska/year: 1970

Description

The body is of medium proportions with the dorsal fin in the center of the back and the adipose (fatty) fin near the tail. The back color is generally a greenish-blue, sometimes shading into purple. An indistinct pink-orange band extends along the sides from head to tail. Below the pink the sides are very light, shading into white on the belly. The back and upper sides are covered with small black spots.

Range

Native to the Pacific coast from northern California to Alaska. Transplanted across the northern United States.

Character

Habits and colors of rainbows vary from one place to another. Some go to sea and then return to their home rivers to spawn. These are steelheads. The times of the river runs may vary from one region to another, so there may be runs occurring in summer, fall, or winter, depending upon the location. In the Great Lakes the runs occur in both spring and fall. Rainbows are not hard biters and often it is difficult to distinguish between a fish and water turbulence.

Location

Rainbows are found in clear, cool streams, rivers, and lakes. In rivers and streams, they prefer holding a position in smooth, moving water at the upper edges of rapids and riffles or behind fallen trees and branches close to the bottom. Except for periods of migration up home rivers, rainbows roam in lakes during the summer. In lakes they remain just under the thermocline at a maximum depth of about 35 feet in warm weather, moving closer to the surface as it cools.

Season

Early spring, late fall, and early winter are the best periods to fish for rainbows on rivers and streams. Early fall is the best season for lake fishing.

Time

Early morning, at dusk, or on cloudy days when it is easier for the fisherman to remain unnoticed by the fish.

Water Temperature Activity Range

47°–67° F.

Food

Emerging insects, crustaceans, small fish, trout spawn

Tackle

SPINNING: Ultralight with 2 to 4 pound test line and 1/16 to 1/4 ounce lures. Lake Michigan and Pacific coast rivers require a medium to heavy 8 to 9 foot rod, with 8 to 14 pound test line and 3/8 to 5/8 ounce lures.
FLYCASTING: 7 to 8 foot rod with No. 5 or No. 6 line. Lake Michigan and Pacific coast rivers require an 8 to 9 foot rod with No. 9 or No. 10 line with large capacity reel to hold backing line in addition to the regular line.
HOOK SIZES: Wet flies: No. 10 to No. 12. Dry flies: No. 12 to No. 18. Bait hooks in Great Lakes from No. 6 to No. 10, larger on the west coast.

Lures

Fly imitations of hatching insects, spoons with some silver, spinners in silver, crayfish and shrimp imitations, large streamers, bucktails. Best lure colors are purple, blue, gray, yellow, black, silver, red.

Baits

Salmon eggs or trout eggs, nightcrawlers, minnows

Methods

Bright spoons or spinners can be fished upstream on rivers and streams where bait fish are common, and the insect hatches limited. Imitations of insect hatches are productive when seasonal hatches are peaking.

In early spring, trout usually feed on the bottom, and at this time worms are excellent bait. The worm must come to the fish as if it were drifting along freely on the river current, so some weight is usually necessary, but it should not be excessive.

Spring is a good time to use spoons and spinners also. Casts are made upstream slightly beyond where the fish might be, and as the lure settles, it has time to get down to where the fish are.

Spawn sack fishing, in spring and fall, is successful with coho salmon and chinooks as well as with rainbows. The sacks should be small, with 3 to 5 eggs in each, and made from nylon or gauze. They are most effective when they are rolling on the bottom, so weight is added in an amount sufficient to keep the sacks down while permitting them to roll.

It is difficult to detect a fish on the line when a spawn sack is in use, so the safest way to fish with one is to set the hook whenever an unusual action occurs.

Fishing with a spawn sack from a boat or while wading can provide the sack with freedom to roll along the bottom. A stationary position has a more limited range and action, therefore reducing the catch.

Before the big insect hatches in the spring, wet flies can be successful. Wet fly action should imitate the actions of pre-adult water insects. After an upstream cast, the fly is allowed to sink slightly as it moves downstream. The movement of the fly can be followed by pointing the rod toward it and by keeping the rod in line with it. Weight can be added to the line if the trout are deep, and plenty of slack can be included in the casts to give the fly the necessary depth. The slack can be taken up as the fly moves in from its upstream position.

In June the insect hatches are at their peaks, and this is the season for using dry flies. Light tackle will do well because the large fish do not feed on the surface often enough to affect the overall fishing. Flies are usually cast upstream and allowed to drift over the trout. The way the fly floats is important; it should be selected for water resistant qualities, such as stiff hackles, tails, non-absorbent bodies, and light wire hooks.

In the early summer during the insect hatches, dry flies can catch trout in lakes on the surfaces. When the surface water cools in the fall, trout can be caught by shallow trolling or casting with spoons or spinners. Spoons and spinners can also be fished deep when the fish are escaping the surface heat. Jigs can also be fished deep or used in combination with a bubble for sub-surface casting.

SUNFISH FAMILY

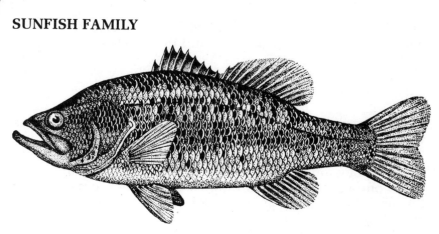

Largemouth Bass

Largemouth Bass   *Micropterus salmoides*

Common maximum weight: 3 lbs./North American record: weight: 22 lbs. 4 oz./length: 32½ in./place: Georgia/year: 1932

Description

The body is compact, moderately deep, and wide. The head and mouth are large with the corners of the mouth extending beyond the eyes. Basic body color is olive green on the back, shading into greenish-silver on the sides and to white on the belly. The spiny dorsal fin in front is connected to the soft, flexible dorsal fin behind it to form a distinctive kind of single fin.

Range

Southeast Canada, south through states east of the Mississippi River system to the Gulf of Mexico. Introduced west of the Rocky Mountains.

Character

Largemouths are sight feeders that sometimes hunt in small schools. Generally they remain hidden among weeds, then lunge forward to attack prey. They are sensitive to the movements of boats, fishermen, and to lure shapes as well as to lure movements.

Location

They are found in shallow lakes or slow-moving waters where heavy weed growth occurs. In spring they can be found in shallow bays where the water is warmer during the day. In summer they move into the shallows early in the evening and move out again in the morning as the water warms. During the day they remain in the shade or in deeper water, but seldom go to water over 20 feet deep.

In the summer in small lakes and ponds, largemouths can frequently be located in the centers close to surface from late afternoon to early morning. They search out small insect-eating fish.

Season

In the north, largemouths can be caught most of the year, except during the coldest months when they become semi-dormant. In the south, they are active all year.

Time

Largemouths apparently feed at any time of the day in shallow or deep water, but they may be more active early in the morning and early in the evening.

Water Temperature Activity Range

65°–75° F.

Food

Crayfish, small fish, frogs, large insects

Lures

Plugs, plastic worms, jigs, grubs, spoons, spinners, bass

bugs, poppers, plastic salamanders. Red and white are preferred colors. Wet or dry flies in combinations of orange and yellow; black and white; red, white, and yellow; green, white, and yellow.

Baits

Nightcrawlers, minnows, crayfish, frogs

Tackle

BAITCASTING: Light or medium, with 6 to 12 pound test line and 1/4 to 5/8 ounce lures.
SPINCAST: Light or medium, with 6 to 12 pound test line and 1/8 to 1/2 ounce lures.
SPINNING: Light or medium, with 6 to 10 pound test line and 1/4 to 5/8 ounce lures.
FLYCASTING: 8½ to 9 foot rod, with No. 7 or No. 8 line, 12 pound test leader.
HOOK SIZES: 2 to 3/0.

Methods

Largemouth bass can be located in shallow water by fancasting or trolling in open spots close to the weed edges. Single-hook lures are best for heavy vegetation, and they should be retrieved the instant they hit the water. Quick starts give the impression of a living creature attempting to seek cover or escape. Jigs can be flipped into openings.

Bass can be found in small lakes and ponds early in the morning and late in the afternoon by starting in the center and circling away from the center toward shore. Surface lures that imitate bait fish, both shallow running or diving, will produce. Poppers and streamers on a fly rod are also effective.

During the day, when bass are more likely to be in deep water, trolling is the fastest method for finding them. A 3-way swivel, a half-ounce dipsey sinker and a No. 3/0 hook can be used with a large floating plastic worm, rigged weedlessly. The sinker is attached to about 18 inches of light leader below the 3-way swivel, and from 12 to 18 inches of line-strength leader is connected from the swivel to the hook. If the sinker gets snagged, the lighter leader will allow loss of the sinker without losing the rest of the rig.

During the trolling, the sinker is used as a guide to water depth as it is bounced along the bottom. When a hit is felt, usually a gentle tug, the boat can be stopped and the tension taken off the line so the fish can get a firm hold on the lure. Then the line is reeled in slowly until the slack is taken up, and the hook is set.

An alternative is to reel in the slack, set the hook after a couple of tugs are felt, and proceed with playing the fish.

In water over ten feet deep, the drag should be released while trolling. It is better to use the drag in water less than ten feet deep, and the hook can be set quickly after a strike.

Spoons without sinkers can be trolled and bottom-bumped in addition to the other method. Sometimes one method will produce where the other will not.

Deep water casting can also catch bass. The lure is cast, allowed to touch bottom, and retrieved slowly. As soon as a tug from any direction is noticed, the hook is set. A variation is to retrieve the lure in steps, bouncing it off the bottom at intervals. If the lure is halted on its fall to the bottom, the hook is set. A fish may be on the line and not be noticed.

Largemouths may strike at different retrieval actions on different days, which would indicate that variations on an unproductive pattern might get results.

In deep water or near bridges or pilings, lures can be dropped straight down and jigged with good results. Strikes usually occur as the lure is falling.

Bottom fishing with a slip-sinker rig and a plastic worm or plastic salamander, rigged weedless, can get excellent results. When a salamander is used as a lure, the hook should be set the instant the slightest touch is felt. (See TROLLING, pp. 54-56.)

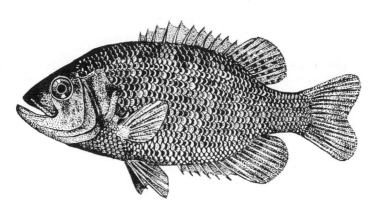

Rock Bass

Rock Bass *Ambloplites rupestris*

Common maximum weight: 1/2 lb./North American record: weight: 3 lbs./length: 13½ in./place: Ontario/year: 1974

Description

The compact body is moderately deep. The spiny front dorsal is connected to the soft dorsal behind it. The basic color is brownish-green, tinged with brassy or dark mottling. Colors change to blend with the bottom structure. The eyes are usually colored a deep red.

Range

Southern Canada through Great Lakes region to New York, west to North Dakota, south to Alabama and Arkansas.

Character

Rock bass are usually found in schools, but in spring the females spawn in shallow water in nests, and the males guard the nests until the eggs hatch. During the year they may migrate a short distance.

Location

Rock bass prefer clear, cool water in lakes and rivers with sand, gravel, or rocky bottoms and sparse vegetation. They remain in about 6 to 15 feet of water, but toward evening during the summer, they may move into shallower water.

Season

All year, but they do not bite well during the coldest months because they become semi-dormant.

Time

All day

Water Temperature Activity Range

65°–75° F.

Food

Aquatic insects, small fish, crayfish larvae, some vegetation

Tackle

SPINNING: Ultralight or light with 2 to 4 pound test line and 1/16 to 1/8 ounce lures.
FLYCASTING: 6½ to 7½ foot rod with a No. 4 or No. 5 line system.
HOOK SIZES: No. 8 to No. 12.

Lures

Wet and dry flies, streamers, small spoons, small spinners, marabou jigs

Bait

Nymphs, larvae, hellgrammites, worms, grasshoppers, crickets, crayfish, minnows

Methods

In lakes, rock bass can be located by trolling with a small spoon or crayfish hooked through the tail, bottom up. The lure or bait should be bottom-bumped. After the school has been located, lures and baits can be cast and bottom-bumped during the retrievals.

At night rock bass can be caught in shallow water during the summer. Surface fishing should be done slowly, with pauses and variations in the lure action.

In rivers, rock bass can be caught close to the bottom near rocks, undercut banks, and in pool areas. A lure can be cast upstream and allowed to sink slowly as it drifts downstream. (See RIVER FISHING, pp. 52, 53.)

Similar Species

Warmouth (Chaenobryttus coronarius)

RANGE: Mississippi basin to the Gulf of Mexico.

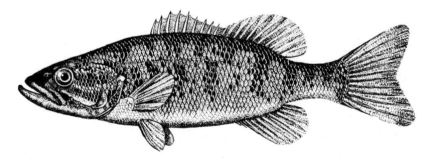

Smallmouth Bass

Smallmouth Bass *Micropterus dolomieui*

Common maximum weight: 2 lbs./North American record: weight: 11 lbs. 15 oz./length: 27 in./place: Kentucky/year: 1955

Description

The body is moderately compact and of medium width and depth. The mouth extends only to the pupil of the eye, unlike the mouth of the largemouth bass which extends beyond the eye. The basic body color is dark golden-green with a brassy-bronze luster. Indistinct vertical bands extend from the back down the sides. The spiny dorsal fin is connected to the soft dorsal fin behind it.

Range

Southern Canada, New England south to Florida, Great Lakes region, upper Mississippi, Ohio, and Tennessee River systems, West Coast.

Character

Smallmouth bass are unpredictable feeders and at times are difficult to catch. The males guard the nests after the females spawn. In lakes, smallmouths wander in schools, but larger bass tend to be somewhat solitary.

Location

Smallmouth bass inhabit lakes and large streams where the water is clear. In lakes during the day, in spring and early fall, they may be found in shallow water, but in summer they tend to stay in deep water during the day and in shallow water from late afternoon until early morning. They congregate along drop-offs with rock, sand, or gravel bottoms.

In rivers, the bass go to riffles and rapids late in the afternoon until early in the morning. During the day they stay in pools near undercut banks, where there is shade, cool water, and a sand or gravel bottom.

Season

May and June are the most productive months, but smallmouths can be caught until the water reaches about 50 degrees. Below that temperature they become semi-dormant and feed very little.

Time

Early morning and late afternoon are best for river fishing, and early morning and early evening are best for lake fishing.

Water Temperature Activity Range

60°–75° F.

Food

Crayfish, small fish, aquatic insects.

Tackle

BAITCASTING: Ultralight or light with 4 to 8 pound test line and 1/8 to 3/8 ounce lures.
SPINCAST: Light or medium with 4 to 8 pound test line and 1/8 to 3/8 ounce lures.
SPINNING: Ultralight or light with 4 to 8 pound test line and 1/8 to 3/8 ounce lures.
FLYCASTING: 8 to 8½ foot rod with No. 6 or No. 7 line.
HOOK SIZES: No. 2 to No. 6

Lures

Small spoons, small spinners, streamers, plastic worms, bucktails, minnow imitations, small poppers, crayfish imitations, small jigs, and bottom insect imitations. Browns and yellows are the best colors.

Baits

Crayfish, grubs, grasshoppers, nightcrawlers, nymphs, mayflies, small minnows, leeches

Methods

In lakes, smallmouths can be located by trolling with a crayfish hooked through the tail, or a minnow. When they have been found, the bait can be changed to a lure. In deep water, bottom-bumping is a favorite method of retrieving casts. (See TROLLING, pp. 54-56.)

Floating plastic worms or minnows rigged with a slip-sinker are productive also. The bass is allowed to run with the bait for 10 to 15 feet, then the hook is set. The bass has time then to get the bait in its mouth.

A 1/8 ounce marabou jig is an excellent lure for smallmouth bass. If the jig is not taken by a fish on the way to the bottom, it is allowed to settle, then it is arced across the bottom. If there is no response, the lure can be cast in another direction and the arcing repeated. An almost unnoticeable jigging action may improve the effectiveness of the lure.

Shallow casts can be made close to logs, bars, and weeds, and in openings where the bottom is covered with rocks, sand, or gravel.

In rivers, smallmouths can be located close to the bottom near rocks, undercut banks, and in pools. Water power provides the action for the lure, so the retrieve should be made slowly. The lure can be cast upstream and allowed to sink as it drifts downstream. Smaller lures are more productive in rivers than large ones. (See RIVER FISHING, pp. 52, 53.)

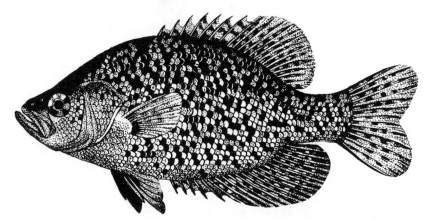

Black Crappie

Black Crappie   *Pomoxis nigromaculatus*

Common maximum weight: 3/4 lb./North American record: weight: 5 lbs./length: 19¼ in./place: South Carolina/year: 1957

Description

The body is compact, deep, and moderately wide. The basic body color is light yellow-green with a tinge of silver. Irregular, broken rows of black scales cover the body, making the black crappie easy to identify. The spiny dorsal fin is connected to the soft dorsal fin behind it.

Range

Southeast Canada through Great Lakes region and Mississippi valley to Gulf states. Introduced elsewhere.

Character

Crappies are school fish that follow shorelines from deep to shallow. In large lakes they may migrate several miles. They are sight feeders, and like other sunfish, the male guards the nest after the female spawns in spring or early summer. Crappies have tender mouths and are not strong fighters.

Location

Lakes and streams near deep water and hard bottoms. Crappies prefer clear water around weed beds, brush, logs, rock piles, sunken islands, drop-offs. They suspend from five or six feet under the surface to just above the bottom, depending on sun position and available shade. Early and late in the day or on cloudy days, crappies will spread out in weedless lakes, but stay within a few hundred feet of a drop-off. In fall when the water cools and the weeds die off in weedy lakes, they will suspend away from the weed line in deep water, but not far from it.

Season

Black crappies are active throughout the year, but early summer and fall are the most productive months.

Time

Any time of day, but best times are early morning and early evening. At midday, deep water and shade will produce.

Water Temperature Activity Range

60°–75° F.

Food

Small fish, aquatic insects, crustaceans.

Tackle

SPINNING: Ultralight or light with 2 to 4 pound test line and 1/16 to 5/16 ounce lures.
FLYCASTING: 6 to 7½ foot rod with a No. 4 or No. 5 line system.
HOOK SIZES: No. 4 to No. 6

Lures

Small spoons, spinners, streamers, spinner-fly combinations, plastic worms, jigs, plugs. Purple and black are popular colors, but light colors are productive also, in pink or white.

Baits

Small minnows, insect larvae, worms, beetles, grasshoppers, crickets.

Methods

Early in the season, crappies can be located by slow trolling with a small crappie jig suspended from a bobber. After vegetation has developed, the jig is more effective with the addition of a small minnow hooked through the lips.

Trolling can begin along weed edges, close to the weeds and shallow, with the depth and distance from the weeds increased with each successive pass. By changing the rod position from one side to another, a wider strip of water can be covered. Change positions at regular intervals on each pass, with the final pass occurring when the bobber is about 20 feet from the breakline.

Once the crappies are located, the boat can be hovered or anchored. Short casts can be made into the school with a jig-minnow combination. Casts can also be made from a slowly moving boat, along the weed edges. If the school is lost in one direction, reverse boat movement and try to find it in the opposite direction.

The sinking speed of the jig should be timed with a count-down. If, for example, the fish hits on the count of 5, the general depth of the school can be determined by the succeeding casts on the same count.

Slow drops are often more effective than faster ones, so rubber grub bodies and tails can be more effective than feather types.

Crappies stay close to vegetation after a cold front comes through. A jig can be dropped directly into the weeds and trolled slowly against the weed edge. The jig should be kept close to the bottom and under the vegetation. Short stretches of trolling can be combined with casting.

Movements and speeds of trolls depend upon water temperature. In cold water minnows should be trolled slowly, and in warm water movements should be speeded up so that the action imitates the darting-resting patterns of a swimming minnow.

Similar Species

White Crappie (Pomoxis annularis)

RANGE: Similar to the black crappie, but is more common to warmer and cloudier waters.

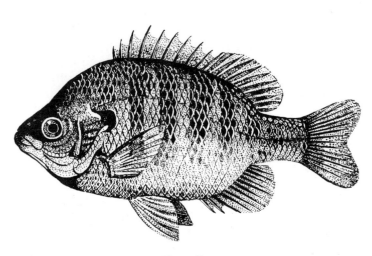

Bluegill

Bluegill   *Lepomis macrochirus*

Common maximum weight: 1/2 lb./North American record: weight: 4 lbs. 12 oz./length: 15 in./place: Alabama/year: 1950

Description

The body is compact and deep. The color ranges from light to dark olive with a purple to lavender luster. The belly is yellow to orange near the gills. The sides have indistinct vertical bands of dark green, shading into burnt orange. The opercular flap (gill cover flap) is broad and colored a deep blue-black. The spiny dorsal fin is attached to the soft dorsal fin behind it. Along with other small sunfishes, the bluegill is one of the most colorful of North American fishes.

Range

New York through the Great Lakes region to Minnesota, south to Georgia, west to Arkansas.

Character

Spawning is done in the spring. During the nesting season, the male guards the nest. At other times, bluegills travel in small schools. They are scrappy fighters when hooked, but they may inspect the bait for a period of time before actually taking it.

Location

Bluegills are found in ponds, lakes, and streams in heavy vegetation. In spring they move into shallow water in bays and channels where they spawn. Large bluegills can often be found near smaller ones, but in deeper water near bars and drop-offs. Bluegills and crappies often suspend.

During the summer months, bluegills can be found in shallow water near vegetation from late afternoon until early morning. But during the day, they remain in deeper water, at weed edges, near bars and drop-offs.

Season

May to October is good. Feeding decreases rapidly with the temperature under 55 degrees.

Time

Bluegills are daylight feeders that hunt by sight. Best times are early morning during the first couple of hours of daylight, and early evening during the last two hours or so of daylight.

Water Temperature Activity Range

65°–80° F.

Food

Insects, small crustaceans, worms, fish fry, some vegetation

Tackle

SPINNING: Ultralight with 2 to 4 pound test line and 1/16 to 1/8 ounce lures.
FLYCASTING: 6½ to 7½ foot rod with No. 4 or No. 5 line system.
HOOK SIZES: No. 8 to No. 12.

Lures

Wet or dry flies, nymphs, plastic worms, plastic grubs, small spinners, green sponge spiders, poppers in yellow and black, yellow and red, white and orange, and leadhead jigs in white or yellow, with a small piece of pork rind dressing.

Baits

Tiny minnows for large bluegills, worms, beetles, insect larvae, crickets, grasshoppers

Methods

In shallow water, splashing and fast bait action should be avoided. Bobbers should be balanced to baits to avoid excessive resistance to the fish. The bait can be drifted over weeds and logs slowly, whether it is fished with a bobber or floating on the surface. Hooks should be set quickly but lightly.

In deep water, weed edges are productive and can be fished parallel or in and out. Split-shot sinkers are the best to use because the bait can be balanced to drop at about a foot per second or less. This gives the bluegill time to take the bait on the descent, and indicates how deep the fish are.

Bottom fishing for bluegills is done with a slip sinker rig and a small minnow or sponge spider as bait.

During the hottest months, large bluegills may be in deep water from 15 feet to 30 feet. At these depths, small jigs of about 3/16 of an ounce will produce.

Bluegill lures should always be moved slowly and occasionally stopped, even in warm water. In cold water, the stops should be extended. (See BACK TROLLING, p. 55.)

Similar Species

Longear Sunfish (Lepomis megalotis)

RANGE: Small streams of the Mississippi valley.

Pumpkinseed (Lepomis gibbosus)

RANGE: Maine to Minnesota, south to Florida and Mississippi valley.

Green Sunfish (Lepomis cyanellus)

RANGE: Central states to Colorado. Introduced elsewhere.

Redear Sunfish (Lepomis microlophus)

RANGE: Mississippi basin, south from Illinois. Common to the south.

Spotted Sunfish (Lepomis punctatus)

RANGE: Ponds and streams of the south.

Bait Fishes

	Preferred Water Temperature
Minnows	68°-72°
Bluntnose	
Fathead	
Shiner	
Perch	68°
Alewives	53°-55°
Cisco	52°-55°
Lake chub *Couesius plumbeus*	49°-52°
Deepwater sculpin	41°-46°

10

Conclusion

Sport fishing is one of the most rewarding of leisure time activities. There is pleasure in shopping for equipment, in planning a trip, in relaxing on the water, and in eating the fish.

Unfortunately, in recent years, some of the pleasures of fishing have been eroded by increased numbers of fishermen, increased competition among fishermen, and over-commercialization. The focus on big-money contests and record catches will not promote the cause of sport fishing. It will, if anything, harm it by changing sport fishing from a relaxed, unpressured, outdoor experience into an aggressive, single-minded pursuit, lacking in both pleasure and sportsmanship.

Only a small percentage of a fish species survive to become trophy-size fish, and heavy fishing pressure in some areas has reduced them to the point where future catches will diminish in both quality and quantity. By eliminating the larger fishes, the best of the breeding stock is also eliminated.

Large fish are not as good to eat as smaller ones, so it would be better for the future of fishing to release them. Careful handling of fish to be released is necessary because any contact of the fish with a dry or rough surface will remove the protective mucous that covers the fish and fungus will develop, insuring a slow death.

The decision to release a fish should be made quickly, before it comes into contact with hands or a net. While the fish remains in the water, its lower jaw can be grasped in one hand (wet, to prevent mucous removal) with the thumb and forefinger, while the other hand removes the hook.

Fish with sharp teeth can often be released by lowering the rod-tip to the water, while working the hook loose with the rod action.

A fish should not be released if it requires handling, or if it has come into contact with hard surfaces or a net.

Unless there is a reason for keeping a large fish, releasing it may be one way, along with habitat preservation, to maintain quality fishing into the future.

Index